DIVING AND SNORKELING GUIDE TO 🐢🐢🐢🐢🐢🐢🐢🐢🐢🐢🐢🐢🐢🐢🐢

The Turks & Caicos Islands

Stuart and Susanne Cummings

Pisces Books™
A division of Gulf Publishing Company
Houston, Texas

Publisher's note: At the time of publication of this book, all the information was determined to be as accurate as possible. However, when you use this guide, new construction may have changed land reference points, weather may have altered reef configurations, and some businesses may no longer be in operation. Your assistance in keeping future editions up-to-date will be greatly appreciated.

  Also, please pay particular attention to the diver rating system in this book. Know your limits!

Pisces Books
A division of Gulf Publishing Company
P.O. Box 2608, Houston, Texas 77252-2608

Library of Congress Cataloging-in-Publication Data

Cummings, Stuart.
    Diving and snorkeling guide to the Turks and Caicos Islands/
Stuart and Susanne Cummings.
        p.   cm.
    Includes index.
    ISBN 1-55992-067-X
    1. Skin diving—Turks and Caicos Islands—Guidebooks.   2. Scuba
diving—Turks and Caicos Islands—Guidebooks.   3. Turks and
Caicos Islands—Guidebooks.   I. Cummings, Susanne.   II. Title.
GV840.S78C84 1993
797.2'3—dc20   92-34115
                                                                          CIP

Pisces Books is a trademark of Gulf Publishing Company.

Printed in Hong Kong

10 9 8 7 6 5 4 3 2 1

Table of Contents

Acknowledgments

We would like to express our appreciation to the following companies and individuals whose extreme generosity with their time, assistance, and cooperation was invaluable to the preparation of this guide:

- Peter Hughes' *Sea Dancer*, Providenciales
- Le Deck Beach Club, Providenciales
- Cayman Airways
- Carnival Airlines
- Cliff Hamilton, Director of Tourism, Turks and Caicos Tourist Board

We extend a very special thanks to the crew of *Sea Dancer* and Art Pickering, owner of Provo Turtle Divers, whose abundant and unparalleled knowledge of their local dive sites is reflected throughout the pages of this guide. We look forward to our next visit to the Turks and Caicos Islands.

The uninhabited island of West Caicos is known for its excellent wall diving and its pristine white beaches.

How to Use this Guide

This guide is designed to acquaint you with a variety of the best and most popular dive sites in the Turks and Caicos Islands and to provide useful information that will help you decide whether a particular location is appropriate for your abilities and intended dive plan. You will find, for example, information on macro and wide angle photography, drift diving, wall diving, shallow reef diving, and much more. In Chapters 3 and 4, you will find a dive-site by dive-site description of the special features of individual sites and information regarding recommended skill levels. The experience levels are repeated in a condensed format at the beginning of these chapters.

Regardless of how you choose to use this guide—either reading it from cover to cover or selecting sections of interest—certain chapters should be viewed as required reading. Chapter 5 on "Smart, Safe Diving" is of primary importance. No matter how much we think we know or remember, we can always benefit from a refresher. The section on "Reef Etiquette and Bouyancy Control" in Chapter 5 focuses on tips to help preserve our fragile marine environment and to be ecologically responsible divers. We hope you'll find that some of the tips in this section will help you make a personal contribution to preserving our delicate reef system and will make you a more skillful diver. If you plan to continue diving into your senior years, wouldn't it be nice to have something beautiful to look at?

Although this guide is directed at people who enjoy spending a substantial amount of time in or under the water, everyone has to come up for air. And because some surface intervals are longer than others, we have tried to give you a brief overview in Chapter 1 of the Turks and Caicos on dry land. If you have been to any of these islands, you obviously enjoyed your stay enough to consider returning. But don't imagine that just because you've seen one, you've seen them all. Each island offers its own unique ambiance, its own distinctive personality. If you have never experienced these islands, get ready for some wonderful discoveries and surprises.

Some snorkeling can be done off the beach in Grand Turk but most of the better snorkeling is accessible by boat.

The Rating System for Divers and Dives

Our suggestions as to the minimum level of expertise required for any given dive should be taken in a conservative sense, keeping in mind the old adage about there being old divers and bold divers but few old, bold divers.

We have rated the dive sites based on the following qualifications: A NOVICE diver is in decent physical condition and has recently completed a basic open water certification diving course by an internationally recognized certifying agency, or is a certified diver who has not been

Whether you dive on a live-aboard or a day boat, there is always a friendly divemaster to lend a hand.

diving recently (within the last 12 months), or is a certified diver who has no experience in similar waters. An INTERMEDIATE diver is a certified diver in excellent physical condition, has been diving actively for at least a year following a basic open water course, and has been diving recently (within the last six months) in similar waters. An ADVANCED diver has completed an advanced certification diving course, has been diving recently in similar waters, and is in excellent physical condition.

If you are not sure which category you fit, ask the advice of a local divemaster or instructor on the island. You will find a list at the end of this guide of all the dive operators on each island. They are best qualified to assess your abilities based on the prevailing dive conditions on any given site. Be honest about your qualifications—diving "over your head" can be an unpleasant and uncomfortable experience. If you're still in doubt, ask a divemaster or instructor to accompany you on the first dive in new waters.

If you haven't been diving for 12 months or more, you and your equipment may need a checkout. Make sure your equipment, especially your regulator, is in top condition. If your skills are a little rusty or you are using new and unfamiliar equipment for the first time, take a refresher dive in the pool with your local dive store or do one when you arrive in the islands with an instructor at the dive center with which you'll be diving.

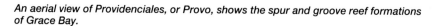

An aerial view of Providenciales, or Provo, shows the spur and groove reef formations of Grace Bay.

1

Overview of the Turks & Caicos Islands

The Turks and Caicos Islands have been referred to as the Secret of the Caribbean or the Isles of June (referring to the most idyllic month of the year). Both are appropriate as this virtually undiscovered archipelago is a paradise where the mild temperatures of June reign eternal every month of the year. But these islands also hold a wealth of delightful sur-

The beach at Northwest Point in Provo, only accessible by boat or four-wheel drive vehicles, offers some interesting snorkeling including an occasional school of squid.

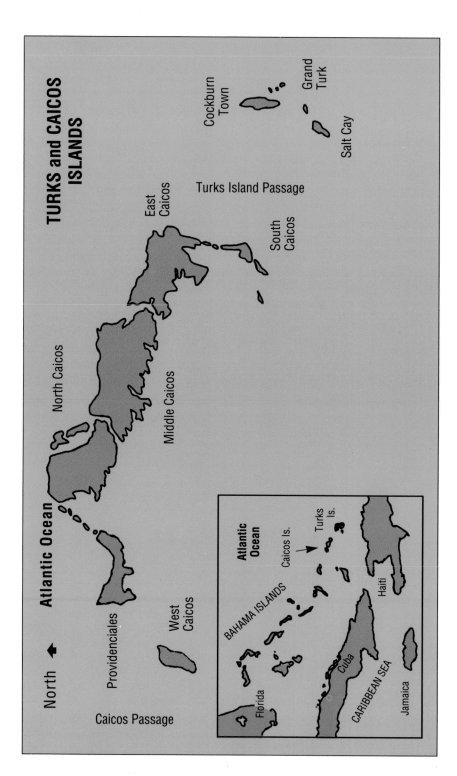

TURKS and CAICOS
ISLANDS

North ←

Atlantic Ocean

Cockburn
Town

Grand
Turk

Salt Cay

Turks Island Passage

East
Caicos

South
Caicos

North Caicos

Middle Caicos

Providenciales

West
Caicos

Caicos Passage

Atlantic
Ocean

Caicos Is.

Turks
Is.

BAHAMA ISLANDS

Haiti

Florida

Cuba

CARIBBEAN SEA

Jamaica

A rusted steam-driven tractor reminds visitors to West Caicos of its once bustling sisal and salt industry.

prises for visitors that range from offshore banking tax benefits to uncrowded powder white beaches and superb scuba diving and snorkeling. Until recently, if you asked someone about the Turks and Caicos, you would likely receive a blank stare. But today, the secret is out. Economic development has taken hold and scuba divers in the know place this destination high on their lists of places to submerge.

History. The Turks and Caicos are a tiny British Commonwealth Colony consisting of 30 small islands (only eight are populated), totaling an area of only 166 square miles. Yet, while the islands may be small in size, their history is rich and captivating. The islands were first inhabited by the Lucayan or Arawak Indians, but their most colorful history begins with their discovery by Christopher Columbus in 1492. During the 1600s and 1700s, they experienced an age of piracy during which they sheltered some of the world's most notorious pirates, including a band of women adventurers called The Bloody Sisters. Overlooked by the European powers who were busy conquering and colonizing larger, lusher islands in the Caribbean's West Indies, the Turks and Caicos remained largely unpopulated until 1668. Two years later, Spain ceded the islands to Britain and, with the arrival of the Bermudian Saltrakers in Grand Turk and Salt Cay, salt became the mainstay of the islands' economy for the next 275 years.

In their more recent past, the Turks and Caicos Islands were a dependency of the Bahamas until 1874 when control was turned over to the

The Turks and Caicos flag flies beside the stars and stripes of the United States.

Jamaican government. In 1962, Jamaica declared its independence and the Turks and Caicos became a British Commonwealth Colony, its current status.

Geography and Climate. The Turks and Caicos Islands are geologically an extension of the Bahama chain, lying at its southernmost end.

The arid climate of the Turks and Caicos Islands is not only ideal for cacti but for divers who enjoy crystal clear waters unmarred by runoff.

They are located 575 miles southeast of Miami, about 90 minutes by air. The 30-mile wide Turks Island Passage runs between two limestone plateaus, one of which forms the Turks Islands that consist of one main island and ten cays and the other, the Caicos Islands with six main islands and 30 cays.

Pearly sand beaches, rich green low-growing shrubbery, arched coconut palms, turquoise waters, and azure skies create a dazzling picture of contrasting colors that would inspire artist and photographer alike. Tidal areas nurture mangroves that in turn create a natural reserve for birds and marine life. On the northern side of the archipelago where the shores abut the Atlantic Ocean, an extensive barrier reef protects the islands and produces an underwater spectacle that challenges the imagination of divers from all over the world.

With gentle, refreshing trade winds tirelessly caressing the islands, the climate is never too hot. Located just south of the Tropic of Cancer, these subtropical islands make an ideal year-round resort. Summer temperatures range from about 90° to 96°F. While humidity may rise to 90%, light winds off the ocean temper the effect. From December to March, the climate averages a cool, dry 75°F, while springtime temperatures vary from 75° to 85°F.

Dress for tropical weather. Casual resort and leisure wear is accepted attire for daytime. Pack a sweater for evening, especially if you are planning to visit during the winter months. Consistent breezes and low humidity occasionally result in the Caribbean's version of a "wind chill factor."

Local Information and Services

Currency. The U.S. dollar is the official monetary unit.

Time Zone. The Turks and Caicos observe Eastern standard time. They observe daylight savings time from April 1 to October 27 as on the mainland.

Postal Service. Letters and postcards to the U.S. require the same amount of postage as in the U.S.

Telephone. Cable and Wireless Ltd. provides national and international telephone, telex, and fax service. You may make international calls by dialing direct or placing the call through an operator.

Banks. Comprehensive international banking services are provided by Barclays and Scotia Banks.

Credit Cards. The majority of hotels and some stores accept American Express, Visa, and MasterCard. Most do not take personal checks. Cash or travelers checks are preferred and recommended, especially on the smaller islands.

Car Rental. Providenciales and Grand Turk have cars, scooters, and bicycles for rent. A driver's license is required. Don't forget to drive on the left-hand side of the road.

Electricity. 120 volts/60 cycles. No plug adaptors are needed.

Tourist Information. For more information, contact the Turks and Caicos Tourist Board, Pond Street, P.O. Box 128, Grand Turk, Turks and Caicos, B.W.I., 800-441-4419 or 809-946-2321, fax: 809-946-2733.

Island Sea Center features an 80-acre marine "pasture" where dolphins participating in the Into the Blue *project are eased into their new environment.*

Island Sea Center

At Provo's Island Sea Center you can learn about the queen conch mariculture project, *JoJo,* the bottlenosed dolphin you may unexpectedly find accompanying you on your dives, and *Into the Blue,* the dolphin rehabilitation program to enable the safe release of dolphins who had previously been in captivity.

Into the Blue, the newest program at the Sea Center, uses the Center's vast and beautiful 80-acre marine "pasture" for its dolphin rescue, rehabilitation, retirement, and release program. Established by an international coalition of conservation and animal welfare groups, *Into the Blue* attempts to acquire dolphins that have been in captivity for all or most of their lives and return them to the wild ocean by providing a transitional and controlled environment where they can learn to become self-sustaining in the ocean. This may entail something as obvious as "deprogramming" a dolphin so he does not "perform" for food or as complex as restoring its health and strength. Three dolphins have recently graduated from the program. They came to *Into the Blue* from dolphinaria in Britain where they had been penned in small indoor tanks. Imagine their excitement at feeling the rain on their backs and seeing the brilliance of the sun for the first time. Today they are cruising the waters around the Turks and Caicos exploring a new and free world.

This is only the beginning. There are over 400 dolphins in captivity worldwide. Perhaps when you dive around Provo, you may just find yourself swimming with an *Into the Blue* graduate. You can identify an *Into the Blue* dolphin by the brand on his dorsal fin. More information about this program is available at the Island Sea Center in Leeward on the island of Provo.

The Islands. Today, the Turks and Caicos are primarily known as a center for offshore banking and diving-oriented tourism. The six main Caicos Islands are separated from the Turks to the southwest by the 7,000-foot deep Turks Island Passage. Most of the people currently inhabiting the islands reside on Grand Turk and Providenciales. Salt Cay and South and North Caicos are also relatively populous. East and West Caicos are uninhabited.

Grand Turk and Salt Cay

Situated at the most northern point of the Turks archipelago, east of the Caicos Islands, is Grand Turk. It is only six miles long and barely a mile wide, the smallest of the Turks and Caicos main islands, yet it has the largest township of any of the islands. Its population of around 5,800 exceeds that of Providenciales, the most rapidly developing island.

For over 400 years, Grand Turk has been the seat of government for the islands. It was originally established by Bermudian Saltrakers, and the Bermudian influence can still be seen in the quaint colonial style architecture of the public buildings and old historic homes. On the west side of Grand Turk is Cockburn Town, the islands' capital since 1766. Founded by Bermudian saltrakers about three centuries ago, Cockburn Town's Front Street is lined with charming 19th-century pastel painted houses. A quaint blending of European and Caribbean flavor creates a distinctively old world feeling. Don't be surprised when you meet one of the local donkeys meandering aimlessly down the street!

Another side of Grand Turk is revealed along its miles of quiet, uncrowded white sand beaches. Not far offshore, numerous deserted cays beckon vacationers to come and explore. Underwater, Grand Turk's wall is world renowned among scuba enthusiasts, attracting divers from all over the world to its treasures and surprises.

If you want to see what the island of Grand Turk looks like in all its splendor, travel from the northeast point where you can visit a photo-worthy lighthouse and a former U.S. Navy base southward along the ridge road. The panoramic view of the whole island with its sparkling anchorages and dazzling beaches is breathtaking.

A mere seven miles southwest of Grand Turk lies the tranquil island of Salt Cay. Spanish and Portuguese explorers as well as English and French

The Imperial Lighthouse located adjacent to an abandoned military base is one of Grand Turk's scenic landmarks and a favorite spot for photographers.

The quiet waterfront streets of downtown Grand Turk offer visitors a taste of old world island charm.

merchant adventurers found their way to this tranquil landfall during the 1500s and 1600s. But it was not until the 1650s when Bermudian traders saw the potential of the island's salt water ponds as a source of profit that Salt Cay was settled. Joshua Harriott, one of the most prominent, and wealthiest of the Bermudian salt traders, built his family's ancestral home on Salt Cay at the beginning of the last century. His large stone White House has endured time and hurricanes and remains the dominant feature of the islandscape as you approach from Grand Turk. On the island, visitors can explore the remains of what was once a carpenter's shop, blacksmith's forge, sail loft, and small boat harbor. There is even ancient salt on the ground floor where it once had been stored by the family.

The salt industry dominated the economy of Salt Cay for centuries. When the salt market collapsed in the 1960s, the emigration of residents left Salt Cay with a scant population of only 200. Today, a visit to Salt Cay is a unique opportunity to step back in time and history. Little has changed since 1900 when the salt industry enjoyed its heyday. A complex system of salinas remains surprisingly intact—one windmill has been restored to working condition—as are many of the buildings and artifacts of the old solar salt industry. Old stone houses now bear fresh coats of paint and colorful bougainvillea create a warm, hospitable atmosphere. Everyone knows everyone and locals are generous with their smiles as you pass them on the road. Quiet bays, superb beaches and quaint Bermudian-style homes with colorful gardens provide a port-of-call for visitors and photographers seeking a haven off the beaten track. Recently, Salt Cay was designated a UNESCO World Heritage site, enabling its unique history and culture to be appreciated and protected for generations to come.

Diving is a fairly new tourist attraction on the island. Dive operators from Salt Cay now take divers to explore local sites as well as those at Grand Turk. Some of Grand Turk's dive boats visit Salt Cay sites as well.

The only accommodations on the island are a handful of charming guest houses that offer an abundance of comfort and casual hospitality.

One of Salt Cay's old windmills that has recently been restored to working condition stands amidst the island's complex of salinas.

Horseback Riding in Salt Cay

If the first image that comes into your mind when you visit the exquisite white beaches of Salt Cay is of a rider galloping on his steed along the duned beach—live your fantasy! Your hotel will be happy to arrange horseback riding for you. Its not only a great way to enjoy the beauty of the island, but it's a great way to get to some of the best snorkeling on the island. So hop on— but don't forget your mask, fins, and snorkel!

Horseback riding along the beach is one way to explore Salt Cay.

Providenciales and West Caicos

On the west side of the Caicos archipelago lies the 38-square-mile island of Providenciales, familiarly called Provo. Twice the size of Bermuda and the largest landmass of the island group, Provo has been transformed from an unknown tropical hideaway to a contemporary and accessible slice of paradise by a group of millionaire developers who obviously knew a good thing when they saw it.

If you had visited Provo in 1964, you would not have found a car on the island. Today, with a growing population and more of a Florida Keys atmosphere than that of other British influenced destinations like Bermuda or Nassau, it has become the center of tourism development in the Turks and Caicos. In recent years, the island has undergone a virtual explosion of new hotels, expansions, and renovations. A number of establishments offer a wide variety of accommodations as well as dive packages with operators on the premises or nearby.

Don't be misled, however, by its rapid growth. Many visitors consider Provo to be the most attractive of these islands. Its 37.5 square miles are also home to gently rippling creeks, protected sounds, tidal flats, and mangroves in the western part of the island and 14 miles of powder white sand beach running the length of the northern coastline. The south coast faces the transparent turquoise waters of the Caicos Bank where Chalk Sound, a national park near Sapodilla Bay, features a shallow pale blue salt lake with two narrow entrances to the Caicos Banks. Its northern coast, protected from the Atlantic Ocean by the barrier reef, offers sublime beaches as well as the island's two oldest settlements, the Bight and Blue Hills. If you want to capture a real Caribbean village feeling, these are worth a sidetrip.

Colorful local fishing boats can be seen along the shore at Blue Hills in Provo.

Hotels, dive operations, a marina and yacht club as well as beautiful beaches can all be found at Turtle Cove on Provo.

JoJo, *Provo's resident bottlenose dolphin, can often be seen playing in the waters along the shore of Grace Bay.*

The old ruins of two plantation houses, stones engraved by shipwrecked sailors, the Hole at Long Bay or, of course, the Conch Farm are also worth including on a land tour itinerary. In addition to scuba diving, deep sea fishing, bone fishing, day cruising, windsurfing, waterskiing, and glass bottom boat trips can easily be arranged on the island.

A short excursion from Provo is West Caicos, an island about the same size as Grand Turk but uninhabited. Pure white beaches stretch endlessly along the eastern and northern shores. You are unlikely to see a footprint unless you make it yourself. In sharp contrast, the western shore is dominated by craggy cliffs that create a dramatic panorama. At one time, West Caicos provided sanctuary for pirates and later, its waters protected U-boats cruising the area. Now, only the remnants of the old sisal and salt industries that operated from 1890 to 1920 hint at its more illustrious history. Its only full-time residents are the wild flamingos, ospreys, and herons that congregate at Lake Catherine in the center of the island. Visitors, however, include avid divers and beachcombers.

PRIDE

Once you explore the Turks and Caicos above and below water, it is easy to understand why its residents are so conscious of preserving the natural resources of these pristine islands. PRIDE, which stands for Protect Reefs and Islands from Degradation and Exploitation, is a nonprofit foundation that was established in 1976 to do exactly that through aggressive conservation education, pragmatic natural resource management, and safe scuba exploration. Among PRIDE's pet projects is the protection of *JoJo,* an Atlantic bottlenosed dolphin who left his pod and swims in the shallow waters of Provo and Pine Cay in the Marine Park since 1980. *JoJo* seems to enjoy human interaction a great deal and often swims with divers and snorklers. If you do meet *JoJo,* PRIDE suggests that you let the friendly dolphin approach you. He'll often stay and play for quite a while. Be careful to keep your hands away from his eyes and blowhole and don't attempt to ride him!

The Other Islands

South Caicos lies 22 miles east of Grand Turk, geographically at the very end of the Caicos chain. At one time an important salt producing island, today it is a queen conch and lobster harvesting center. Cockburn Harbour, its only settlement, was once used by pirates because the narrow harbor allowed them total control of the entry into the port. It is the only natural harbor in the Turks and Caicos and the site of the annual South Caicos Regatta. South Caicos is at its most picturesque at beautiful Belle Sound and along the ridgeway of Sail Rock Hill where you can see a panoramic view of the fringing reefs, the Turks Island Passage, and the bonefish flats of the Caicos Bank that extend for over 40 miles to Provo.

Middle Caicos may be the largest of the Caicos Islands, but its population of 400 makes it the least developed of the inhabited islands. Nevertheless, there is plenty to see. Miles of beaches, large freshwater lakes, lush pine forests, and an extensive network of caves at Conch Bar entice visitors. The coastal scenery at M'djan Harbor is striking. In the small settlements of Lorimers, Bambara, and Conch Bar, you'll enjoy a warm welcome from the fisherman and farmers living there.

East Caicos, once the center of a flourishing sisal industry, is now uninhabited except for the wild cattle that graze there. Accessible only by boat, its miles of beaches are ideal for the adventurous beachcomber.

For centuries the bread basket of the islands, North Caicos was once known for its fine sloops built to carry crops from its farms near Bottle Creek, Whitby, Sandy Point, and Kew to neighboring islands. Beautiful beaches can be seen along its northern coast and fishing enthusiasts will find its creeks full of schooling bonefish and tarpon.

Accommodations. Throughout the Turks and Caicos, visitors will find a variety of tourist accommodations with the greatest concentration in Provo and Grand Turk. Provo is the only island with large resorts, but you will find small intimate inns, condo colonies, small hotels and guest houses on all of the inhabited islands. A number of charter and live-aboard dive boats also offer accommodations.

Entertainment. Island cooking, continental cuisine and, of course, fresh seafood, dominate the bill of fare at many of the islands' restaurants. But if your tastes run to Mexican, Italian, Oriental and Jamaican— or even pizza, you won't be disappointed. Restaurants tend to be casual. You can find any kind of ambiance from the intimate and romantic to something lively or dining by the sea. Many restaurants don't take credit cards, so if you aren't prepared to pay by cash or travelers checks, call and check on the restaurant's policy before you go.

Cayman Airways is one of the commercial carriers that offers regularly scheduled service from Miami directly to the Turks and Caicos Islands.

The Turks and Caicos Islands offer a wide selection of accommodations from full-service resorts to intimate beachside hotels such as Le Deck in Provo.

Shopping. The Turks and Caicos are not for those vacationers who live to shop. On the other hand, you can find some wonderful local handicrafts and tourist goods at the retail shops at the dive operations and hotel boutiques that carry a good selection of resort wear, postcards, t-shirts, and sundries. There are a few small shopping centers, especially on Provo, but no major duty-free stores—so far. Liquor is a good buy with reasonable prices and good selections of hard-to-find island brands as well as popular name brands.

Day Tripping. The best way to see the island on which you're staying is by car. Cars can be rented at typical island rates on the inhabited islands. You can also rent scooters and bicycles in Provo and Grand Turk. Taxis are available as well. Most hotels will be happy to arrange small boat excursions for you.

If you would like to see the islands by air, several air charter companies will custom design an island-hopping tour for you. It is an ideal way to explore all of the islands of interest during the limited time of your vacation. Flying on the scheduled national airlines that serve all of the settlements is an excellent way to make the acquaintance of some of the local residents.

Recreation. As with most island paradises, in the Turks and Caicos, water sports are the order of the day—every day. Whether you choose to go fishing, on a sailing excursion, windsurfing, snorkeling, or scuba div-

> ### *Snorkeling at Smith's Reef*
>
> Not far from Turtle Cove is Smith's Reef, a shallow 25-foot deep patch reef located inside the barrier reef surrounding Grace Bay. Lushly decorated coral heads rise from the sea bottom to about 5 feet below the surface. It is a perfect spot for a warm-up dive. But don't expect it to be uneventful just because it is shallow—small turtles, eagle rays, vibrant tropicals and even a placid nurse shark may join you for a morning romp or a night dive. It's unquestionably one of Provo's best snorkeling sites.

ing, water is abundantly accessible—especially for diving, which is one of the main attractions of these islands to visitors. Reef and bonefishing are also popular throughout the islands with the majority of excursions based in Provo.

Transportation. One of the best things about the Turks and Caicos is that they are easily accessible and not very far away from the U.S. mainland. Major commercial airlines offer regularly scheduled service from Miami to Provo and Grand Turk. Check with your travel agent or Turks and Caicos Tourism Board for information on airlines servicing these islands.

Regularly scheduled inter-island air service between the main islands including Provo, Grand Turk, Salt Cay, South Caicos, Middle Caicos, North Caicos, and Pine Cay is available on Turks and Caicos National Airlines and Charles Air Service.

Customs and Immigration. U.S. and Canadian visitors don't need a passport, visa, or innoculations to enter the Turks and Caicos, but you must have some form of positive identification to prove citizenship such as a birth certificate, voter registration card, or photo ID. Citizens from other countries do need a passport and, in some cases, a visa. Absolutely no spearguns are permitted in the islands, and they may not be brought through customs.

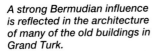

A strong Bermudian influence is reflected in the architecture of many of the old buildings in Grand Turk.

2

Diving in the Turks and Caicos Islands

Frontiers are hard to find these days. But if you relish the opportunity to experience incredible walls that are lush and clean, pristine coral gardens alive with colorful tropical fish, and large pelagics cruising the walls, sooner or later you end up in the Turks and Caicos. Clearly, for underwater excitement, activity, and diversity, the Turks and Caicos are among the few frontiers remaining in the Caribbean.

It is not uncommon to see dolphins riding the bow of your boat, whales migrating through the Turks Island Passage in the winter months, turtles exploring the reefs along with divers, or manta rays somersaulting off the wall. This is what makes the marine environment one of the Turks and Caicos' most precious natural resources.

Until recently, the Turks and Caicos remained a secret except to private pilots and the small number of businesspeople who appreciated the benefits of this modern day tax haven. Today, tourism has caught hold. But, much to their credit, citizens of Turks and Caicos have taken early steps to protect their marine assets. The Princess Alexandria National Park, the first of 33 land and sea parks within the country, now has moorings installed at various sites to protect the reefs from damage caused by boat anchors.

With the establishment of the Watersports Association of the Turks and Caicos Islands (WATCI), an excellent selection of highly capable and knowledgeable dive operators and three live-aboard dive vessels that cruise throughout the islands, the diving opportunities in the Turks and Caicos Islands only promise to grow.

Diving Conditions. Due to the arid climate and minimal rainfall, there is little sediment running off into the surrounding waters. The visibility is almost always good, frequently superb, and the reefs are healthy

Divers will be impressed by the miles of pristine walls and healthy coral growth that greet them in the Turks and Caicos Islands. ▶

The 110-foot Sea Dancer *is one of four live-aboard dive vessels that cruise the Turks and Caicos Islands.*

and clean. In fact, there are few places left in the Caribbean where reliably excellent visibility can almost be guaranteed. Visibility generally ranges anywhere from 60 to 150 feet plus. Water temperatures are around 75° to 79°F in the winter months and 80° to 85°F during the summer. Wetsuits are recommended for winter diving.

On the northern side of the archipelago, where the shores touch the Atlantic Ocean, an extensive barrier reef nearly 50 miles long protects the islands and produces an underwater spectacle that challenges the imagination of divers from all over the world. You never know what may be swimming just above or below you or 50 yards off the wall. Look around you in all directions when you're swimming along the walls and the reefs. You may just come up from your dives with some real fish stories! And if you happen to be visiting these islands during February and March, you might even spy a humpback whale or two as their migrating pods pass through the Turks Island Passage between Grand Turk and South Caicos every spring.

The Turks and Caicos may not be known as a shopping mecca, but visitors to some of the islands' small shopping centers such as the Marketplace in Provo will discover an array of gifts and local handicrafts to bring home. ▶

Diving in Grand Turk and Salt Cay

While some are drawn to Grand Turk for its offshore finance advantages and others to enjoy the miles of tranquil beaches, it is the renowned wall that draws divers from around the world. Here, along the west coast with its nearby walls, you will find the very best diving in Grand Turk. To describe the diving as lush is to understate the reality.

In addition to reefs and walls that are among the best in the Caribbean, Grand Turk diving has some unusual advantages. First, the water is usually calm because the wall runs parallel to the island on the leeward side with protected waters and excellent visibility. Second, because the wall is only about 300 yards from the shore, boat rides to all of the dive sites are brief. Finally, because the wall begins at an average depth of 35 feet, the dives are generally accessible to divers of all levels, and you have substantially more bottom time on the wall than on most wall dives that tend to begin deeper.

Guests staying on Salt Cay can visit the sites at Grand Turk as well as Salt Cay. While diving around Salt Cay is only beginning to expand, new sites are being explored all the time. Some of the sites already have permanent moorings, and access is quite easy with a local dive operator.

In Grand Turk, only a quarter of a mile or less offshore, the wall begins at only 25 to 45 feet and plunges to 7,000 feet.

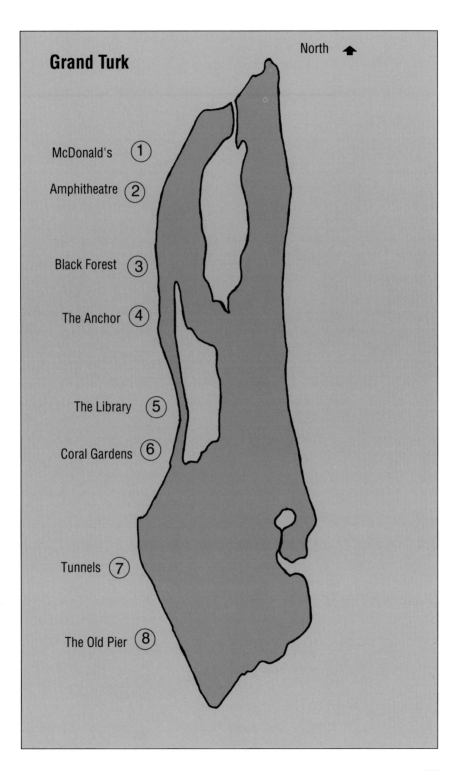

Grand Turk

North

McDonald's (1)

Amphitheatre (2)

Black Forest (3)

The Anchor (4)

The Library (5)

Coral Gardens (6)

Tunnels (7)

The Old Pier (8)

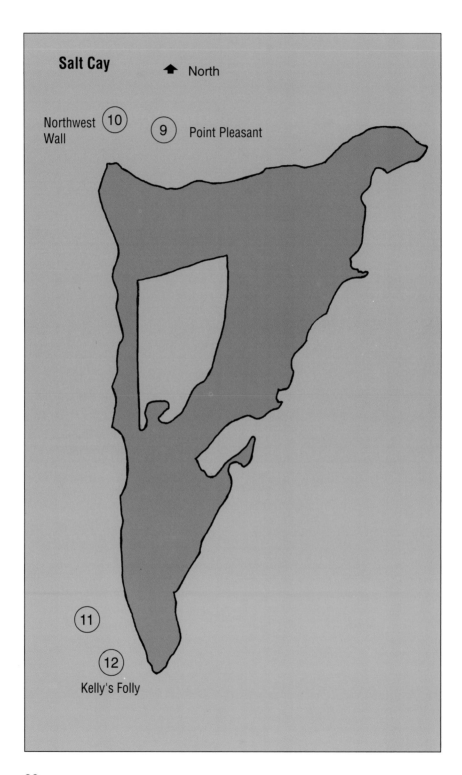

Salt Cay

North

Northwest Wall (10)

(9) Point Pleasant

(11)

(12)

Kelly's Folly

Salt Cay also offers excellent snorkeling and shallow diving just off-shore. Huge reefs of elkhorn coral rise to the surface from the sandy floor 20 feet below. Colorful tropical fish dart among the dense configurations of varied hard corals and gorgonians. Dive sites are located on the southern and northern ends of Salt Cay. The eastern coastline tends to be defined by rugged limestone sculpted by wind and water, while the leeward shore on the western side of the island displays a collection of seawalls, docks, and jetties where local boats can easily land.

At both Grand Turk and Salt Cay, during the summer months, watch for manta rays and dolphins who play along the shallows near the wall. In winter, humpback whales come within sight of the shore during their annual migration. Snorkelers visiting Grand Turk will discover two things—first, conditions at the good sites vary with the season and, second, many of the best snorkel sites are only accessible by boat. If you would like to experience the best of Grand Turk's snorkel opportunities, contact one of the local dive operators on the island and he will be happy to point you in the right direction and arrange a snorkel charter for you if necessary.

Dive Site Ratings

		Novice Diver	Novice Diver and Instructor/Divemaster	Intermediate Diver	Intermediate Diver and Instructor/Divemaster	Advanced Diver	Advanced Diver and Instructor/Divemaster
Grand Turk							
1	McDonald's	x					
2	Amphitheatre		x				
3	Black Forest		x				
4	The Anchor		x				
5	The Library		x				
6	Coral Gardens		x				
7	Tunnels		x				
8	The Old Pier	x	x				
Salt Cay							
9	Point Pleasant	x					
10	Northwest Wall		x				
11	Black Coral Canyon		x				
12	Kelly's Folly		x				

Columbus Landfall

Where did Columbus land first? We may never know the truth, but some new studies maintain that Christopher Columbus may have touched the shores of Grand Turk after his long voyage in 1492. According to Gonzalo Fernandez de Oviedo y Valdes, whose account of the journey was published 43 years after the discovery, his description of cays south of the Discovery Island seem to match those south of Grand Turk Island. He states that Columbus stayed between the Island of Guanahani and another called Caicos. In Columbus' own logbook and letters, the explorer positions his Discovery Islands in relation to the north coast of Hispaniola exactly as Grand Turk is positioned. The controversy continues to rage on—what do you think?

Just a short swim from Salt Cay's northern shore, snorkelers will discover a lush marine world in only 15 feet of water.

McDonald's 1

Typical Depth Range:	30 to 130 feet plus
Typical Current Conditions:	Slight tidal
Expertise Required:	Novice with instructor
Access:	Boat

This is an excellent dive site. Because of its lush coral display of soft and hard species and stunning formations, a return dive is often requested by first time visitors. Below the mooring is a sandy area in 25 to 30 feet of water where divemasters used to feed the fish regularly. Currently, fishfeeding is strongly discouraged because the fish were becoming aggressive and harassing visiting divers. However, divers will find the fish friendly and curious. This area is home to a variety of grouper, queen triggerfish, a pair of immense gray angels and every photographer's pet peeve, the "Caribbean Piranha," a theatrical yellowtail snapper who seems, more often than not, to put his nose or tail into everyone's photos! You may even see a turtle or two here. Scattered coral heads are worth exploring for small critters.

As the sandy area slopes down to 50 feet, divers will come upon the most prominent feature at McDonald's, The Arch, after which the site was named (McDonald's Golden Arches). This is an excellent source for macro photo subjects. You can swim through The Arch and come out at 70 feet.

On the wall at about 100 feet is a collection of colorful sponges that make the wall look like a painting. From this point, the wall drops straight down to 7,000 feet in the Turks and Caicos Passage. To the right of The Arch as you go from shallower to deeper water is an immense orange elephant ear sponge on the left. On a coral plateau at 50 to 70 feet, you will find a wide variety of fish including schooling grunts, goatfish, and occasionally, a scrawled filefish.

If you enjoy pretty hard and soft corals, give yourself some time to take in the ones on the top reef during a leisurely swim back to the boat at the end of your dive.

Although fishfeeding is actively discouraged now, formerly hand-fed groupers at McDonald's are quite friendly and attentive.

Amphitheatre 2

Typical Depth Range: 30 to 130 feet plus
Typical Current Conditions: Moderate
Expertise Required: Novice with instructor
Access: Boat

On the northern end of Grand Turk not far from McDonald's is Amphitheatre, named for its large sandy amphitheater. At Amphitheatre the reef begins in about 30 feet and slopes to 40 feet before dropping to a sandy gully at 65 feet.

Inshore it is surrounded by patch reefs. The shallower area on the reef is often used for warm-up dives. It is also a good spot for photographers shooting macro. Garden eels, parrot fish, and stingrays inhabit the sandy

Orange elephant ear sponges provide splashes of vibrant color on the wall near Amphitheatre.

Just around the corner from the crack on the wall at Amphitheatre, divers will find this stunning cluster of purple tube sponges that protrude from the vertical facade.

section leading to the reef that abuts the lip of the wall. Sand chutes divide large sculptured coral formations, undercut near the sand where vibrant sponges and tunicate colonies thrive.

Between the first two coral islands, divers will discover a coral archway. Divers can swim through the arch and emerge out on the wall at 80 feet for a very dramatic view of the wall.

The vertical wall begins at 40 feet and is highlighted by great black coral trees, deep water sea fans, purple tube sponges, and a large crack in the wall. A coral buttress that rises to within 30 feet of the surface forms a giant amphitheater that slopes to a cut in the wall that then plunges to 7,000 feet. From a sandy bottom at 40 feet and turning north along the wall with its cut-ins, ledges and overhangs, divers enter the large sand amphitheater surrounded by flourishing coral. It is truly an apt stage for the humpback whales that have been sighted in season.

Stingrays, barracuda, and turtles are found here. In addition to the occasional humpback whale that has been sighted during migration season, divers have even seen a hammerhead shark! A wide variety of invertebrates, such as orange ball anemones, nudibranchs, tunicates, as well as moray eels and octopus make night diving on this site exciting.

Late winter and early spring are whale migration seasons, so keep a sharp eye out toward the blue water off the wall.

Black Forest 3

Typical Depth Range:	40 to 130 feet plus
Typical Current Conditions:	Little to none
Expertise Required:	Novice with instructor
Access:	Boat

Several dives in Grand Turk leave indelible impressions. This is one of them. Black Forest features a dramatic undercut area of the wall that is blanketed by vibrantly hued encrusting sponges and five different varieties of black coral. The wall begins at 50 feet and drops vertically actually undercutting for an expanse of about 100 yards wide. This wall is at its best between 60 and 90 feet. As many as 100 black coral trees grow on this undercut. Because the undercut area is sheltered from the customary surge action that comes with the winter seas and summer storms, the corals and encrusting sponges are unusually healthy and lush. The top of the wall features an assortment of hard corals and some coral rubble including some small stands of pillar coral and a varied community of tropical fish. Don't forget to say hello to the resident barracuda who lives here and reliably makes his appearance to give divers the once-over.

At 100 feet deep, the wall buttresses out in a sloping fashion down to the vertical wall to depth. Near the base, several large orange elephant ear sponges make an excellent wide angle subject.

A night dive on the lip of the wall at Black Forest should produce some interesting photos of octopus that frequently make an evening appearance.

Even though there is plenty of natural light during the day, it is a good idea to bring a dive light with you. In this way, you will be able to discover and enjoy the natural colors of the black coral and beautiful sponges at depth.

This is also a great night dive for more advanced divers. Octopus, moray eels, giant West Indian spider crabs, orange ball anemones, and bright orange tubastrea in full bloom are in abundance on the wall. This dive site is worth more than one visit to do it justice.

The area has, unfortunately, experienced a natural cycle of silting that has caused some deterioration of the black coral. Divers should make a special effort not to touch anything or stir up the silt excessively and cause further deterioration.

It is hard to pull yourself away from this dive site, and therefore it is an ideal first morning dive when you have maximum bottom time and can leisurely enjoy the beauty around you.

A dive light is handy to have on dives at Black Forest because the wall undercuts so much it is often heavily shadowed until later in the afternoon.

The Anchor 4

Typical Depth Range: 40 to 130 feet plus
Typical Current Conditions: Slight to none
Expertise Required: Novice with instructor
Access: Boat

At this site, a large coral-encrusted anchor makes an ideal subject for photographers with a wide angle setup. The old anchor sits atop the reef in 40 feet of water not too far from the lip of the wall. It is so popular a photo subject and, indeed, so photogenic, that it has appeared in magazine articles, brochures, and even on the front cover of the 1983 Turks and Caicos Islands telephone directory!

Divers who keep an alert eye out all around them might be lucky enough to spot one of the reef's many shy creatures like this hawksbill turtle.

A lettuceleaf nudibranch slowly edges its way along the coral at The Anchor.

As with any special feature that many divers wish to enjoy, be considerate and don't stir up the sand and silt around the anchor. Also take care to avoid damaging the encrusting growth on the anchor by kicking it with your fins or grabbing onto it to support yourself.

On the bottom near the anchor in the sand, pearly razorfish, sand tilefish, garden eels, and bluehead jawfish dart in and out of their holes. They are extremely shy, but if you sit quietly on the sand, you will eventually be rewarded by a curious head emerging to look around.

The wall descends vertically at first but quickly assumes a gentler angle until 70 feet where it again resumes its vertical plunge. The soft corals on the wall make a colorful tapestry that stands out from the blue water. At about 100 feet due south of the anchor, a small gully cuts in on the wall and is home to a large school of grunts and snapper.

Eagle rays are often sighted at The Anchor cruising the blue beyond the lip of the wall.

Typical Depth Range:	25 to 130 feet plus
Typical Current Conditions:	None
Expertise Required:	Novice with instructor
Access:	Boat

Most divers unanimously consider The Library one of Grand Turk's premiere dive sites—especially at night. Just off main street of Cockburn Town, across from the old Grand Turk Library, is a wall dive that starts in only 25 feet of water and undercuts to over 100 feet where it abuts a ledge. Not surprisingly, it is called The Library.

It is an ideal dive for novice divers because the wall starts so shallow new divers can experience wall diving without going very deep. For those who haven't been diving for a while, it is also a good site for a warm-up dive.

The terrain is basically a flat, rocky reef that leads to a sheer wall. Along the lip of the wall is an abundance of activity. Scattered around the

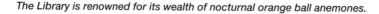

The Library is renowned for its wealth of nocturnal orange ball anemones.

reef are ballast stones shrouded with encrusting coral, a vestige of the salt raking years when salt ships would anchor in Grand Turk.

During the day, schools of grunts and snapper abound, but the magnificent enchantment of this dive site reveals itself at night. One of the best night dive sites anywhere in the Turks and Caicos Islands, and the entire Caribbean for that matter, when the sun goes down The Library blooms with brilliant orange tubastrea, variegated Christmas tree and feather duster worms, violet-eyed arrowcrabs, octopus, puffers, and a density of orange ball anemones that will send tremors through the most seasoned underwater photographer. Divers have boasted of finding as many as 49 on a single night dive before their bottom time ran out! It is a favorite spot of photographers because of its large population of marine invertebrates.

This is a great night dive even for less experienced divers who can stay on the shallower part of the wall. Several local dive operators run night dives to The Library at least once a week. This night dive should not be missed.

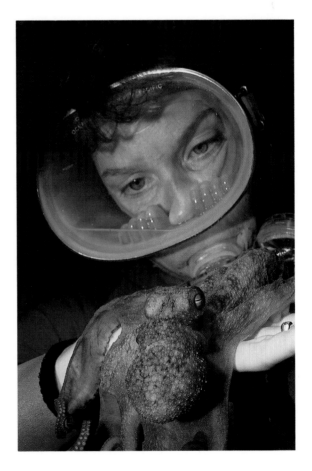

A baby octopus befriends a diver on a night dive at The Library.

Typical Depth Range: 35 to 130 feet plus
Typical Current Conditions: Slight
Expertise Required: Novice with instructor
Access: Boat

When the boat ties up to the mooring at this site, divers will drop down on Coral Gardens, a rolling pasture-like coral-carpeted plateau in 35 feet of water. Horse-eye jacks congregate around the mooring. At the base of the mooring, several sandy basins surrounded by hard corals gently rise to the edge of the wall at about 55 to 60 feet.

Schools of snapper, grunts, and small barracuda hover along the rim of the wall that slopes steeply on a mini-wall from 40 feet to a plateau at 70 feet. Here three sandy bowls surrounded by plate coral, brain and mountainous star coral dominate a landscape accented by small coral heads. Turtles are often found cruising along the wall. In the springtime, divers have reported seeing as many as 15 hawksbill and green turtles at this site on a single dive. The lower plateau slopes down to 90 feet before dropping vertically to the sea floor at 7,000 feet.

Night dives are often done on the reef just below the mooring where the corals and their nocturnal inhabitants emerge to feed.

The top of the wall at Coral Gardens is a good place for fish photography because of the wide variety of species found here.

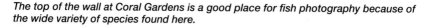

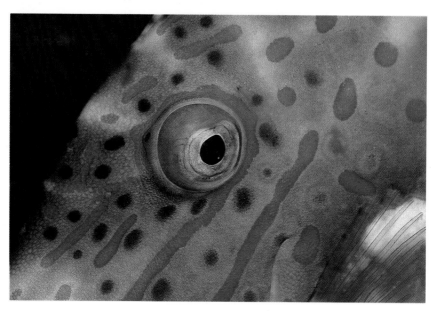

Running just south of the mooring at Coral Gardens, divers will encounter a beautiful stand of pillar coral and an orange vase sponge.

To make the most of your bottom time, begin your dive on the lower plateau, continue to the mini-wall, and finish the dive by exploring the coral area beneath the boat and mooring. There is sometimes a slight current, so check before you enter the water. Swim to the site against the current and return to the boat with it.

Schools of spotted eagle rays cruise the wall each morning at Eagle's Nest in South Caicos.

South Caicos

Divers who have been fortunate enough to submerge at such spectacular sites as Eagle's Nest, Amos' Wall, The Arch, and the Airplane Wreck will attest to the fact that South Caicos offers one of the most rewarding dive experiences available in the Turks and Caicos. Fabulous walls provide the dramatic backdrop for cameo appearances by magnificent pelagics that play along the dropoffs. It is not unusual to see schools of eagle rays, huge loggerhead turtles, and sharks. Unfortunately, as of this writing there is no dive operation on the island or a live-aboard that visits on a regular basis. But keep your ears and eyes open for future developments. South Caicos—when you can get to its truly awesome sites—is not to be missed!

Typical Depth Range:	30 to 100 feet
Typical Current Conditions:	Slight
Expertise Required:	Novice with instructor
Access:	Boat

If you want a site with interesting coral structures, an abundance of hard and soft coral and a wide variety of fish life, Tunnels is an excellent place to submerge.

Tunnels starts inshore of the wall at about 35 feet and emerges on the outside at 80 feet. The sandy areas attract southern stingrays and an occasional flying gunard. Two sand chutes that run a distance of about 80 feet from the top reef at 40 feet to the wall create a coral buttress that forms the lip of the 7,000-foot deep wall. Black coral and gorgonians accent its southern side.

In summertime, somersaulting manta rays are occasionally sighted at Tunnels.

On the southern edge of Tunnels, black coral and gorgonians grow thickly.

Two parallel tunnels extend from the base on the wall at 100 feet to 50 feet inside of the reef, which slopes gradually upward to 35 to 40 feet. Emerging from the tunnels, the expanse of the wall is ablaze with richly colored schools of blue chromis, creole wrasse, snapper, jacks and luxuriant corals, black coral trees, and gorgonians. If you turn southward, you'll discover another smaller tunnel that will return you to the inshore side of the wall. Occasionally huge jewfish have been seen in this smaller tunnel—so be ready with your camera! At the Tunnels, the wall starts at 35 feet. A large tunnel begins inside the reef at 60 feet. Divers who follow the tunnel will emerge outside on the wall at 80 to 100 feet, where they will come upon a sudden outcropping covered with purple tube, huge elephant ear, barrel and vase sponges, gorgonians and schools of jacks. In the summer months, lucky divers may glimpse a feeding manta ray, as this seems to be one of their favorite feeding spots when the plankton blooms. As many as five at a time have been seen here.

Just beneath the tunnel is a small cave that usually houses a school of silversides. At 100 feet, a plateau extends out from the wall that is covered with gorgonia and orange elephant ear sponges.

If you want to siwm through the tunnels, choose the larger one—to the north. It is larger inside and easier to get through. Be careful not to stir up the sandy bottom and ruin the visibility for other divers who want to enjoy it.

The Old Pier (South Dock) 8

Typical Depth Range:	10 to 25 feet
Typical Current Conditions:	Some surge
Expertise Required:	Novice
Access:	Beach or pier

Although it may not look appealing at first glance, like many old trash-strewn piers in the Caribbean, Grand Turk's Old Pier is a great dive. This is a macro photographer's dream. The abundance of surprises below will certainly impress you. And because it is a shallow dive, you have lots and lots of bottom time.

The pier is a steel dock that was built in the mid-1960s to handle shipping needs for the island as well as the construction of a U.S. missile tracking station that was used to track Mercury space shots. As with most piers, this one serves as a garbage dump for the boats and crews that have docked here. Everything from beer cans, tires, fenders, cables, chains, and tableware have found a final resting place at the bottom. But amidst the rubbish and rubble, you'll also find a plethora of creatures who have found the ideal camouflage here.

The smooth trunkfish is one of a wide variety of small tropical fish divers may encounter at Old Pier.

Look around the pilings and grassy areas surrounding the pier for lizardfish, seahorses, octopus, flying gunards, squid, arrow crabs, peppermint shrimp, decorator crabs, and several types of moray and snake eels. Occasionally you may find a frogfish blending almost undetectably into the sponges on the pilings. Batfish are fairly common around the shallow end of the pier, but they blend in well and can move surprisingly fast if they feel harassed. All of these creatures maximize their environment and you can easily swim past them without noticing, so look carefully around you. On the other hand, don't touch, prod, or harass the creatures. This is their home and you are merely a visitor.

During the summer months, manta rays also frequent the area around the pier and the adjacent beach. They have been seen most often in the afternoons.

Two more words of caution—locals fish off this pier and you can occasionally find yourself tangled in clear monofilament line. This is especially important to be aware of at night. It is a good idea for you or your dive buddy to bring a dive knife along just in case. Also, postpone your dive if there is a large freighter unloading and be alert for smaller craft that cruise the area especially when you are ascending.

At the time of this writing, another newer, larger pier is under construction in Grand Turk. In time, it too will attract its share of marine inhabitants and may be a worthy dive site.

If you look carefully, you will find well camouflaged creatures such as this lizard fish at The Old Pier.

Typical Depth Range:	5 to 15 feet
Typical Current Conditions:	Tidal which can be strong
Expertise Required:	Novice
Access:	Boat or shore

At the northern end of the island is Point Pleasant, a shallow dive with a maximum depth of 15 feet and huge coral heads that rise to the surface with huge stands of elkhorn coral. A surprisingly varied collection of marine creatures play amid the swimthroughs and overhangs, and it is not unusual to see southern rays, stoplight parrotfish, tiger grouper, French angels, African pompano, and schooling blue tang. Keep an eye out for an occasional eagle ray, nurse shark, squid, or the resident tarpon who frequents the area. The site is also accessible from the beach and is an excellent snorkel, one of the best in the Turks and Caicos. If you plan to do any horseback riding along this beach near this site, bring your snorkel gear with you.

Huge stands of elkhorn coral jut to the surface at Point Pleasant.

Northwest Wall (Salt Cay)

Typical Depth Range:	45 to 120 feet
Typical Current Conditions:	None
Expertise Required:	Novice with instructor
Access:	Boat

Nearby at the northwest point of Salt Cay is Northwest Wall where the near vertical wall begins at 45 to 50 feet and plunges to about 120 feet. The reef is covered with pillar coral, sea plumes, sea whips, and star and brain coral while the wall flaunts an abundance of large, healthy deep sea gorgonians, tube and barrel sponges, and twisted rope sponges. The highlight of the site is a coral-covered 25-foot pinnacle at 110 feet that emerges from the wall dramatically and provides an ideal opportunity for wide angle photography.

Black Coral Canyon (Salt Cay)

Typical Depth Range:	35 to 110 feet
Typical Current Conditions:	None
Expertise Required:	Novice with instructor
Access:	Boat

At the south end of Salt Cay, Black Coral Canyon features a steep canyon that begins at 35 feet. Gorgonians and black coral trees are prolific on the south side of the canyon only. At 110 feet where the canyon bottoms out, a big undercut adorned with wire coral and purple and yellow tube sponges sometimes shelters a nurse shark.

The unusual markings of the scrawled filefish make them a colorful subject for photography or video.

Kelly's Folly (Salt Cay) 12

Typical Depth Range:	35 to 100 feet
Typical Current Conditions:	None
Expertise Required:	Novice with instructor
Access:	Boat

Just south of this site is Kelly's Folly. The top of the reef at 35 feet is colorfully decorated with soft and hard corals. An undercut canyon drops off to about 60 feet at a 50° angle but the best diving is near the lip. Marine life is active at this site with everything from spotted morays and hawksbill turtles to hog snappers, grouper, queen triggers, queen angels, grunts, blue tangs, and parrotfish.

Elegant stands of pillar coral decorate the top reef at Kelly's Folly.

4

Diving in Providenciales and West Caicos

Provo is the second most populous of the Turks and Caicos Islands, yet it is experiencing the most rapid growth and development. In fact, the pace of development on the island has been so intense in recent years that the current population is not known for certain. Much of the development is related to an emerging and burgeoning dive industry. And the diving is well worth the visit.

Northwest Point is about a half hour boat ride from Provo. Here the sites along the wall are dramatic and blanketed with healthy marine growth.

The very best diving is at West Caicos where the walls rival any in the Turks and Caicos Islands. Situated ten miles southwest of Provo, West Caicos is about the same size as Grand Turk. The boat trip from Provo's Sapadilla Bay is about an hour to an hour and a half depending on the weather and sea conditions but the voyage is well worth it.

The walls at Provo's Northwest Point are some of the finest in the Turks and Caicos.

Butterfly fish can be seen at almost every dive site throughout the Turks and Caicos.

The "wild west" may be an apt description of this isolated and uninhabited nine square miles of landfall. Topside, the island's west coast is dotted with photogenic inlets, but it is what lies below sea level that makes it one of the favorite destinations of Provo's dive operators. Superb diving along its two miles of wall begins less than a quarter mile from the beach. Along this wall that plunges from 45 to 6,000 feet, the visibility is reliably 100 feet or more.

Currently, there are moorings at West Caicos to accommodate large vessels such as the liveaboard dive boats that take divers to the area. In a further effort to protect this beautiful underwater area, plans are in the works to install moorings for small day boats as well.

Dive Site Ratings

Provo (Northwest Point)	Novice	West Caicos		Novice
1 Canyons	x	9 Land of the Giants		x
2 Shark Hotel	x	10 Midnite Manta		x
3 Black Coral Forest	x	11 Highway to Heaven		x
4 Amphitheater	x	12 Elephant Ear Canyon		x
5 Mystery Reef	x	13 Gully/Sponge Gallery		x
6 The Crack	x	14 Rock Garden Interlude		x
7 The Stairway	x	15 Driveway		x
8 Hole in the Wall	x	16 White Face		x
		17 Sunday Service		x
		18 Isle's End		x

Diving in Grace Bay

Not all of the dive sites around Provo require long boat rides. Right offshore from some of the island's biggest resorts on the north shore of Provo is Grace Bay. The bay is dotted with several good dive sites for divers of all levels and all preferences.

Wreck divers will enjoy a 60-foot deep visit to the 80-foot long cargo freighter *Southwind,* which sank in 1985 and is now frequented by Nassau groupers and schools of horse-eye jacks. It is one of the few sites where fish feeding and petting the friendly groupers is not discouraged. Another wreck, the *We,* is an ideal deep dive for more experienced divers. In 1988, this 110-foot freighter was sunk by local dive operators on a 60-foot deep shelf. Unintentionally, it slid off the shelf into a gully off the wall where it now lies in 160 feet of water with its wheelhouse at about 140 feet. Still intact, it is now home to a community of groupers as well as a huge jewfish estimated to weigh between 300 to 400 pounds.

The crescent-shaped coral head that marks the Aquarium makes a good first ocean dive and snorkel site because the top of the coral head is in 20 feet of water, and divers are likely to see a school of barracuda and a host of varied reef fish. The north shore also offers sites with walls and reefs to explore such as Sellers Cut Wall, Grouper Hole, Long Canyon, Pinnacles, and Fifi's Folly. Local dive operations located on Grace Bay offer regularly scheduled trips to these and other sites in the area.

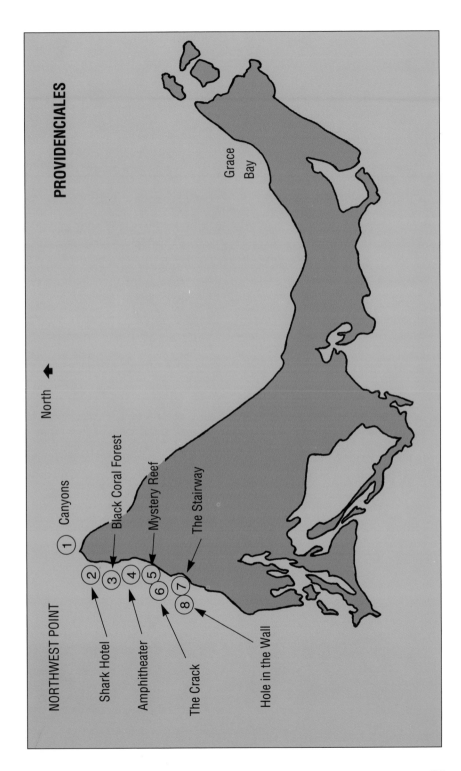

PROVIDENCIALES

North

Grace
Bay

NORTHWEST POINT

Canyons

① Canyons

Black Coral Forest

Mystery Reef

The Stairway

② ③ ④ ⑤

⑥ ⑦

⑧

Shark Hotel

Amphitheater

The Crack

Hole in the Wall

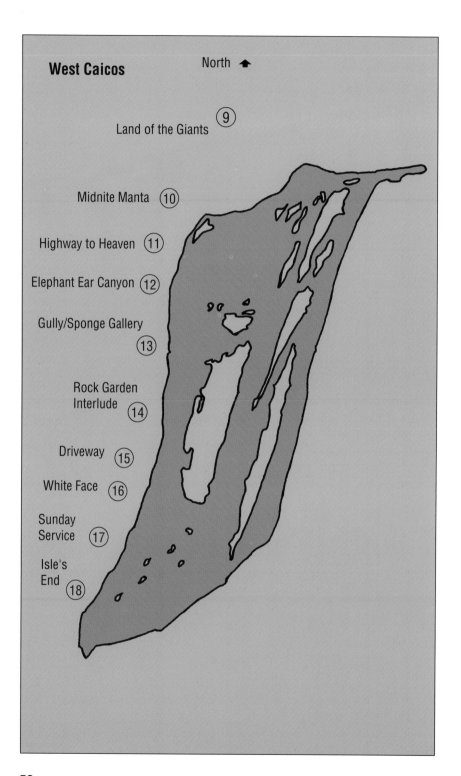

West Caicos

North ↑

Land of the Giants ⑨

Midnite Manta ⑩

Highway to Heaven ⑪

Elephant Ear Canyon ⑫

Gully/Sponge Gallery ⑬

Rock Garden
Interlude ⑭

Driveway ⑮

White Face ⑯

Sunday
Service ⑰

Isle's
End ⑱

The dive sites at Grace Bay are ideal for everything from open water training dives to a convenient afternoon submersion.

Typical Depth Range:	40 feet at top; 65 feet in gullies
Typical Current Conditions:	Some current most of time
Expertise Required:	Novice with instructor or divemaster
Access:	Boat

This dive site is a lot of fun to explore. The terrain is a series of monumental ravines or big valleys—one after another. There are holes, caves, swimthroughs and arches that will keep even the most blasé diver fascinated for the duration of his or her bottom time. One arch is about 25 to 30 feet long and divers can swim through it as long as they do it one at a time.

Marine life is not a strong point of this dive site, although sometimes you will find creatures, especially nurse sharks, in the ravines. In fact, this site is full of potential surprises—you never know what you may find around the next corner! On the tops of the ravines, sea fans, sea whips, and sea plume abound, giving way to diverse hard corals that form small ledges and overhangs. It is within these natural hiding places and shelters that you are likely to find turtles, sharks, lobster, big grouper, and snapper.

There is some current most of the time on this dive site because it is located at the point, and the current tends to sweep around with more strength than at sites further away. The best way to avoid the current is to stay in the valleys where the current generally is not as strong. The strength of the current will also vary with the tide. Check it out before you enter the water and plan your dive accordingly.

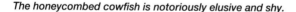

The honeycombed cowfish is notoriously elusive and shy.

Shark Hotel 2

Typical Depth Range:	45 to 110 feet
Typical Current Conditions:	None to slight
Expertise Required:	Novice with instructor or divemaster
Access:	Boat

Shark Hotel is a visually stunning dive that was originally found and named by Art Pickering, who pioneered much of the diving in the Provo area and who owns and operates one of Provo's oldest dive centers, Provo Turtle Divers. Unlike most of the dive sites at Northwest Point where a current is always evident and sometimes strong, at Shark Hotel, the current is virtually nonexistent although you may encounter some choppy seas during the winter months.

A large yellow barrel sponge grows off the wall at Shark Hotel.

This site lies just north of Amphitheater. At the top of the wall near the lip, schools of grunts, snapper, and goatfish can always be found playing. If you want to try some fish portraiture, approach very slowly and be patient. It may take a while for the fish to become accustomed to your presence, but persistence pays off.

The wall begins at 45 to 50 feet and briefly drops straight down to 80 to 100 feet where a coral plateau juts out or buttresses like a shelf before plunging vertically to the depths. This ledge extends for a few hundred yards and is covered by very pretty rope, tube, barrel, and vase sponges with colorful wire corals wending their way through the cracks along the wall. There are also big formations of sheet coral. Near the base of the mini-wall is a chimney-like passage that leads from the top of the plateau onto the lower wall just below the lip of the buttress. The exit on the wall is deep at about 130 feet, so keep an eye on your depth and bottom time.

It is a good place to spot small reef sharks and black tip sharks. You won't be disappointed by the overall reef life either, which is quite prolific. When looking for sharks at this site, it helps to be one of the first buddy teams in the water and over the wall. Rubbernecking is mandatory on the wall!

On your way back to the boat, take a moment to enjoy the huge regal stand of pillar coral under the boat and mooring. They are as large as any you will see in the Turks and Caicos. This area is good for inexperienced divers who are not ready for deeper diving.

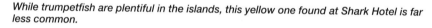

While trumpetfish are plentiful in the islands, this yellow one found at Shark Hotel is far less common.

Typical Depth Range:	45 to 130 feet
Typical Current Conditions:	None to moderate; tidal
Expertise Required:	Novice with instructor or divemaster
Access:	Boat

Situated between Shark Hotel and Amphitheater, the wall itself is the essence of this dive. You won't want to waste precious bottom time on the top reef, so head directly for the wall, which begins in 45 feet of water.

Schools of jacks and an occasional larger pelagic visitor inhabit the top of the wall, which plunges steeply to 130 feet. The best diving seems to concentrate between the top of the wall down to about 80 or 90 feet.

On the face of the wall, there are several undercut sections, one of which displays good examples of densely interwoven red rope sponges that add to the color of the already coral-encrusted facade. This is also a good place to see tunicate colonies that dot this section of the wall.

At 80 feet in another undercut or amphitheater-like formation, you will find an oversized orange elephant ear sponge. Although not as massive as the gargantuan specimen in West Caicos, this is still an excellent subject for some close focus wide angle photography. You'll see another stunning elephant ear sponge nearby at 95 feet.

Two other interesting features of this dive are a coral buttress decorated in deep sea gorgonia and a nearby crevice lined with black coral. According to Bob Gascoine who owns and operates the liveaboard diveboat Aquanaut, this crevice often conceals "something big." Check it out!

Black coral trees veil the edge of an undercut on the wall at 100 feet at Amphitheater.

Amphitheater 4
(Also called Harvest)

Typical Depth Range:	50 to 120 feet
Typical Current Conditions:	None to 1 knot with tidal flow
Expertise Required:	Novice with instructor or divemaster
Access:	Boat

This site is a favorite among divers visiting the Provo area. Amphitheater is part of a spur and groove formation at Northwest Point in Provo. Aside from the sizable stand of pillar coral situated near the mooring under the boat, the interest on the top reef focuses primarily on the fish life. There is not a great deal of coral on the top reef—some coral rubble and scattered sponges—but fish abound. Horse-eye jacks, loads of fairy basslets, goatfish, schoolmasters, black durgeon, barracuda, spot finned, banded and four-eye butterfly fish as well as rock beauties can be found cruising the lip of the wall. Just below the edge of the wall, you'll discover beautiful black capped basslets as well.

From the edge of the reef, the wall drops vertically to an amphitheater formation that undercuts 10 to 15 feet to a sandy bottom at 85 feet. Black coral decorates the upper rim of the undercut. A large orange elephant ear is among the most prominent features of the amphitheater. Red and

A large orange elephant ear sponge spans an undercut section of the wall that forms the Amphitheater.

orange encrusting sponges provide accents of color. Wire coral, rope and antler sponges hang down everywhere. In front of the amphitheater, a protruding buttress exhibits beautiful examples of healthy plate corals, scattered purple tube sponges, and black coral trees. Finally the wall terraces to about 120 feet.

If you plan to do photography in this area, watch your bubbles rising beneath the undercut. They tend to disturb the surrounding silt on the wall, and you'll find clouds of particles falling in front of your lens. To avoid this, move away from the wall to exhale. Also, be aware of your fins—if you inadvertently stir up the fine silt in the small bowl of sand at the base of the amphitheater, you'll not only ruin the visibility but your photo opportunity as well.

Near Amphitheater at 90 feet, is a spectacular display of orange rope sponges that are rare in the Turks and Caicos.

Typical Depth Range:	45 to 130 feet
Typical Current Conditions:	None to moderate; tidal
Expertise Required:	Novice with instructor or divemaster
Access:	Boat

Don't expect to learn the origin of the name of Mystery Reef—it seems to be a mystery to everyone! While the area under the mooring and the boat is sandy, the top reef near the wall is composed of hard corals, coral rubble, and isolated coral heads. There is more coral on this

A trio of barrel sponges provides a dramatic subject for wide angle photography at Mystery Reef.

top reef, in fact, than on many of the other dive sites in the vicinity. A friendly grouper can often be found patrolling the top reef along with a school of horse-eye jacks. On occasion, divers have seen turtles and spotted drums. You can always be assured of finding a wide variety of marine creatures including orange filefish, white spotted filefish, four-eye and banded butterfly, yellowfin grouper, black durgeons, Spanish hogfish, blue striped and French grunt schools, barracuda, and yellowtail snapper.

If you look around the reef carefully, you might locate one of the many cleaning stations established on the reef. Here, minute gobies and juvenile Spanish hogfish can be seen darting in and out of the mouths and gills of tiger grouper, rock hinds, coney, and snapper, removing unwanted parasites.

The dominant feature on this site is an enormous 10-foot-tall stand of pillar coral that perches regally at the top of the wall at about 55 feet. Star and plate coral, purple tube sponges, a few small barrel sponges and vase sponges create a lovely image of color and texture as the wall plunges straight down to 120 feet. Part of the wall here drops sharply while another portion descends more gradually, so watch your depth here and your available bottom time for that depth.

Keep a sharp eye out when you are swimming along the wall. You may just see a large pelagic who has stopped by for a closer look at the strange fish in scuba.

It takes a sharp eye to spot this tiny neon gobie that rests on a brown tube sponge near a feeding station.

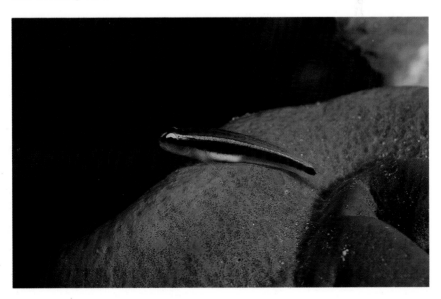

Typical Depth Range:	50 to 105 feet
Typical Current Conditions:	Tidal
Expertise Required:	Novice with instructor or divemaster
Access:	Boat

The Crack is named appropriately for the steep crevice that cuts from about 50 to 100 feet. The terrain at this site is varied. A sand channel marked by a large stand of pillar coral near the boat leads the way from the mooring and the dive boat to the top reef, which averages about 50 feet. Here divers will see a sand bowl and elongated coral heads as well as schooling schoolmasters, mackerel, and grunts.

In The Crack itself, large grouper and snapper tend to congregate. Black coral trees and deep water gorgonia cling to the sides of the crevice.

The wall offers the most diverse topography, however, featuring buttresses, fissures, undercuts, terracing coral, and even a pinnacle that extends off its face at 105 feet. Plate coral and wire coral are plentiful on the wall. A pretty anemone sits on the edge of one of the buttressing sections of the wall, while a sizable barrel sponge marks the 95-foot depth. Lots of entwining rope sponges dangle precariously from small undercut areas. Barrel sponges and several photogenic clusters of vivid purple tube sponges, some as long as three to four feet, catch the cruising diver's eye. At 105 feet on the sloping wall sits a large coral head with ever more nooks and crannies to explore.

For the fearless, a whitetip shark has often been seen cruising the top of the wall, and you never know when he might pay another visit. Again, the diver who keeps looking all around is most likely the one who will see the occasional surprise visit—like a humpback whale, shark, or eagle ray!

Two divers are captivated by the dense sponge and coral growth on the wall at The Crack.

The Stairway 7

Typical Depth Range:	60 to 115 feet
Typical Current Conditions:	Tidal
Expertise Required:	Novice with instructor or divemaster to intermediate
Access:	Boat

This site was named by long-time Provo resident and dive operator, Mary Pickering. The Stairway is essentially a series of coral buttresses indented with deep cuts or crevices starting in the 60- to 90-foot range and bottoming out between 90 to 115 feet. On the top of the wall, the reef

Deep on the wall, a diver stops to admire some heavily entwined purple and yellow rope sponges.

is formed by densely packed hard corals and a soft coral garden. At the beginning of one of the cuts, divers will discover a chimney-like structure. Small to medium-sized barrel sponges, brown antler sponges, and brown tube sponges along the top and sides of coral buttresses dot the seascape.

While you may occasionally spot an eagle ray, Atlantic spadefish cruise the area as well as schooling snapper, tiger and Nassau grouper, yellowfin grouper, black durgeons, butterfly fish, and angelfish. If you look into some of the cuts and under the overhangs, you might find lobsters hanging out.

On a night dive at The Stairway, a photographer gets close enough to capture on film the eye and gill of a sleeping southern stingray.

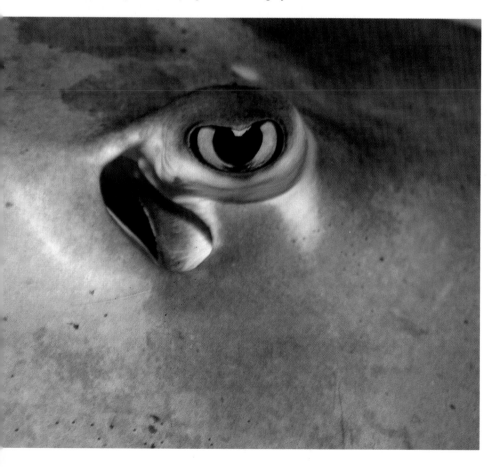

Typical Depth Range:	40 to 90 feet
Typical Current Conditions:	Tidal
Expertise Required:	Novice with instructor or divemaster
Access:	Boat

As the name of the dive site attests, the main feature of this area is a large crack in the top of the coral plateau at 55 feet. The crack or hole dips vertically into the reef, turning and allowing you to emerge on the face of the wall at 95 feet. Only one diver can swim through at a time, but the sensation of finding yourself on the reef one moment and at the endless blue expanse of deep water off the wall the next is truly exciting. Although you cannot see the exit from the entry point, no light is necessary because the other end of the passage will come into view as soon as you complete the vertical descent. It helps to enter the opening and pause for a moment to allow your eyes to adjust before swimming through. In order not to stir up passage for other divers, tuck your gauges in your B.C. and kick with small movements.

In addition to the fun of the Hole in the Wall, the extensive sheet coral formations on the wall are strikingly beautiful. Schooling grunts, snapper, barracuda, and a few moray eels are usually in the area for fish portrait photographers.

When you approach the schooling fish, move slowly or the school will scatter and you'll be without a subject. Take a few minutes to hang inconspicuously around the fish to enable them to get accustomed to your presence. Little by little you can move in closer until you get the setup you want.

At Hole in the Wall, a pair of matching feather duster worms adds a decorative touch to the coral.

A colorful queen angel cruises in and out of the coral on the reef at Hole in the Wall.

Pine Cay

For Provo-based divers, nearby Pine Cay is often on dive operators' itinerary for local dive trips. A privately owned island with a resident population of only 25, this is the ultimate in privacy—no cars, telephones, television, or radio to interrupt the tranquility and natural environment. Its nature trails and pristine beaches are the exclusive reserve of the island's private club and its guests, but the fringing reefs are available to everyone including scuba divers.

Divers will discover a diversity of sea life amid valleys and canyons, coral heads, and ravine-like channels situated side by side. Only a 45-minute boat ride from Provo, these sites are often visited by the Provo dive operators because Pine Cay's visibility seems to be good even when local Provo conditions are marginal.

Typical Depth Range:	30 to 130 feet
Typical Current Conditions:	Mild to moderate tidal flow
Expertise Required:	Novice with instructor or divemaster
Access:	Boat

On the extreme northern end of West Caicos is the Land of the Giants, a steeply undercut wall beginning at 40 to 45 feet and plunging into the bottomless depths. A splendid vision of abstract sculpture covered with hundreds of black coral trees, deep water sea fans, and encrusting sponges, this is unquestionably one of our favorites sites in the Turks and Caicos.

The reef area below the boat and under the mooring lies in 20 to 30 feet of water gradually descending to the top of the wall. In this relatively shallow area, there are numerous undercut rock formations that shelter local marine inhabitants and vibrantly colored encrusting corals and sponges. In the sandy area nearby, divers will find a swimthrough.

Thick formations of antler sponges drape the steep wall at Land of the Giants.

67

A diver closely examines some yellow tube sponges at Land of the Giants.

At 40 feet, the wall begins and slopes to about 70 feet where it undercuts to a shelf at 140 to 150 feet. Hard coral formations, basket sponges, deep sea gorgonians, black coral trees, and luminescent azure vase sponges line the top of the wall, while barrel sponges and wire coral dominate the undercut.

As for Land of the Giants, suffice it to say it was named for the giant sea creatures that tour its wall! Look all around you when you swim along the wall. In addition to the requisite lobsters hiding in the cracks, queen angelfish, Nassau grouper, pink hogfish, porcupine fish and schools of horse-eye jacks can be found. Eagle rays, nurse sharks, and black tip sharks might just surprise you!

Because of the proximity of the Turks and Caicos Banks to this section of the wall, the current and visibility are greatly affected by the tide at this particular spot. On the outgoing tide, the water becomes greener and is accompanied by a tidal current that pours out and down over the wall. It is highly recommended that divers do this dive on an incoming tide. Your chances of seeing big ocean critters will be enhanced as well because the visibility will be better.

Typical Depth Range:	45 feet to depth
Typical Current Conditions:	Slight to moderate; tidal
Expertise Required:	Novice with instructor or divemaster
Access:	Boat

This is another very good dive for novices and an excellent night dive. A patch reef of scattered coral heads and plate coral accented by stands of pillar coral lead to a wall that begins as shallow as 50 feet and angles down far less abruptly than at many of the other sites around West Caicos.

Giant Caribbean spider crabs, lobster, and green moray eels inhabit the nooks and crannies on the top reef. Nurse sharks find shelter amid the coral heads. Off the wall, eagle rays and even a manta ray may be spotted.

At night, the reef virtually comes alive as octopus, crabs, and lobsters emerge to scavenge among the coral heads. In the magic of the darkness, delicate orange ball anemones extend their tentacles, basketstars unravel to reach out for nourishment, colorful shrimp play among the sponges and soft corals. This is the best time to shoot fish portraits because your normally skittish subjects sleep in a semiconscious state wrapped safely in their nighttime cocoon.

This site was named because a ten-foot manta ray used to frequent this spot nightly. It was apparently attracted to the bright lights of the live-aboard *Sea Dancer* during night dives. Who knows—maybe you will be the one to spot him next!

Although manta rays are not found on every night dive at Midnite Manta, the diversity of marine life will impress most divers.

Typical Depth Range:	45 feet in the sand to 70 feet at top of wall
Typical Current Conditions:	Tidal if any
Expertise Required:	Novice with divemaster or instructor
Access:	Boat

Highway to Heaven lies on the north end of West Caicos just south of Land of the Giants. The dive begins in 50 feet of water. The sandy area beneath the mooring and the boat reveal cautious garden eels, but the site is renowned for the southern stingrays that play in the sand, unusually large schools of jacks, and lush healthy soft and hard corals that provide color and texture to the reefscape. A deeper dive at 80 to 100 feet, Highway to Heaven is one of West Caico's best with large coral archways and swimthroughs, big marine creatures, and frequent sightings of reef sharks.

Two prominent, steep sand "highways" are punctuated by towering coral heads. One is accented by a small coral archway, surrounded by gaily-colored schooling fish, that is cut deeply into the top reef at about 95 to 100 feet. The wall drops steeply from the buttresses. These sand chutes create large coral heads and buttresses that begin around 60 feet, slope as deep as 110 feet, but average 70 to 75 feet. One of the smaller coral heads features several overhangs and undercuts on its shore side as well as an arch that divers can swim under, while a large coral head signifies the top of the wall with a rim of gorgonians and black coral trees. Chimney sponges and plate coral also dot the top reef.

As for big marine life, chances are good that you may see a bull or blacktip shark cruising in the deeper water off the wall, if you happen to be one of the first buddy teams to hit the water.

Highway to Heaven is a good place to find the luminescent azure vase sponge that is rare in the Turks and Caicos.

Typical Depth Range:	55 to 100 feet
Typical Current Conditions:	Tidal if any
Expertise Required:	Novice with divemaster or instructor
Access:	Boat

Located north of Gulley and south of Highway to Heaven, you will know you have arrived at Elephant Ear Canyon by the colossal 10.5-foot by 10.5-foot orange elephant ear sponge for which the site was aptly named.

The mooring is situated over a sandy area that all but conceals a wonderful community of elusive garden eels, stingrays, sand tilefish, and margates. Crossing the sand toward the wall, the top reef lies between 55 to 60 feet and is divided into three accessible sections separated by sand chutes. A school of goatfish patrol the area on a regular basis. One part of the reef drops to a mini-wall marked by a large anemone at 65 feet. The mini-wall then slopes more gently to another anemone at 90 feet and a striking black coral tree.

The most dominant feature of the site is, of course, a huge elephant ear sponge that measures more than 10 feet in diameter. Unquestionably one of the most popular sites in West Caicos, you won't forget the awe-inspiring experience of coming upon this gigantic sponge that adorns the

Elephant Ear Canyon is well-known throughout the Turks and Caicos for its enormous 10.5 feet by 10.5 feet orange elephant ear sponge.

The spot-fin butterfly fish is one of several types of butterfly fish seen in the Turks and Caicos.

inside of a canyon-like formation virtually covering the mini-wall at the crest of the cut at about 100 feet. A hard coral is growing out of the middle of the sponge and it almost looks like an enormous orange flower. The canyon is formed by steep valleys surrounded by plate corals and black coral trees. Black jacks can be seen playing among purple tube sponges.

Remember that this sponge is a rare phenomenon of nature, so don't touch it because what you touch, dies. This sponge has taken hundreds of years to grow to this size and hopefully it will continue to flourish for hundreds more to come. Also, the bottom of the canyon where the giant orange sponge sits is covered by a soft fine sand. Try to avoid kicking up the sand—it is not healthy for the sponge and it ruins the visibility for other divers who want to enjoy the spectacle.

If you follow the sand chute down to another bowl-like area at 100 feet, a black coral tree makes another superb wide angle photograph. Between the elephant ear sponge and the black coral tree, you'll find a brown tube sponge at 95 feet on a mini-wall that slopes off to the deep— one more good photo opportunity. With its sponges and black coral trees, this is a superb site for wide angle photography, and photographers shooting fish portraits will find plenty of subjects among the resident Atlantic spadefish, horse-eye jacks, turtles, grouper, schooling goatfish, and margates.

Because the main features of this dive are fairly deep, begin your dive by heading directly for the 100-foot-deep exotica and work your way back toward the top reef at the end of your dive.

Gully/Sponge Gallery 13

Typical Depth Range:	55 to 107 feet
Typical Current Conditions:	Tidal if any
Expertise required:	Novice with divemaster or instructor
Access:	Boat

Sandwiched between Rock Garden Interlude to the south and Elephant Ear to the north, lies Gully where the wall begins at about 50 feet.

Just below the mooring, divers descend to a sandy area scattered by small isolated coral heads. A brown tube sponge in this vicinity marks the location of a cleaning station. Photographers and videographers will find some interesting subjects here as local residents await their turn much as we do when we have our cars washed!

The top reef is a coral garden that begins in 55 feet of water. The principal feature of this site is a gully-like passage that practically severs the

Big brown tube sponges, which are common in the Turks and Caicos, protrude from the wall at Gully.

reef into two distinct sections that slope gradually down toward large buttresses before dropping to the wall. A school of grunts can often be seen cruising this reef area.

Regardless of which section you choose to explore, you will find a host of soft corals and sponges, especially along the lip of the wall where soft coral bushes, deep sea gorgonians and black coral trees mark the point of vertical descent. On one side of the Gully at the point where the cut opens widely, a large barrel sponge and azure vase sponge mark a depth of 100 feet. Slightly shallower, a small grove of delicate black coral trees lies on the other side of the gully at 70 feet. On the other side of the reef, a mini-wall begins at 95 feet and undercuts at 105 feet to form a buttress rimmed by graceful deep sea gorgonians. The wall then plummets to the sea bed at 6,000 feet!

As divers move down the sheer drop, undercut walls are shrouded with encrusting sponges while black coral trees veil long purple tube sponges. A swimthrough at the top of the wall emerges through a tunnel off the wall at about 89 to 90 feet and brings divers to the gully, which is formed by two pinnacles that extend from the wall.

In addition to the friendly Nassau groupers who will be happy to make your acquaintance at the Gully, schooling fish including schoolmasters, mackerel, tiger groupers, permit, margates, and goatfish are common here.

Schools of grunts and snappers are found all along the lip of the wall in West Caicos.

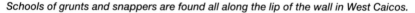

Typical Depth Range:	40 to 120 feet
Typical Current Conditions:	None
Expertise Required:	Novice with instructor or divemaster
Access:	Boat

Rock Garden Interlude is aptly named because it looks a bit like a rock garden—only with coral rather than rocks. The top reef ranges from about 40 feet near the mooring to 60 feet at its deeper points and is divided into two sections by a sand channel. Isolated coral heads decorate the reef and you'll see some beautiful star and brain corals. The coral heads reveal a wide variety of small creatures, and photographers will discover ample opportunities for macro work.

These six-foot purple tube sponges photographed at Rock Garden Interlude have graced the pages of several dive magazines.

Squirrelfish are one of the easiest fish in the ocean to photograph.

These scattered formations also provide an interesting playground for sand tilefish as well as cruising schoolmasters, schools of jacks and Atlantic spades. Grouper, angelfish and a few varieties of butterfly fish, which mate for life and always travel in pairs, also frequent the area. As you swim across the reef, you might come upon an old anchor embedded in the coral.

From the lip of the reef where schools of blue chromis and creole wrasse play among the purple rope sponges, the wall drops vertically to 80 feet and then terraces more gradually to 110 to 120 feet. Just below the edge of the wall, a pair of highhats have taken up residency. Excellent examples of large plate coral can be seen on the vertical portion of the upper wall as well as antler sponges, wire coral, large purple and brown tube sponges, black coral trees, and an occasional orange elephant ear sponge.

Below 80 feet, the slope resembles a dramatic modern painting dominated by red, yellow, and lavender sponges. Keep a sharp eye out for the occasional shark, spotted eagle ray, or turtle that may be swimming by. A large anemone sits at the base of the sand chute that separates the drop-offs. If you have a camera with you, ask your dive buddy to model for a close focus wide angle shot.

As you return to the dive boat, look for flying gunards and southern stingrays in the sandy areas beneath the boat.

Hiking on West Caicos

Take off your fins and mask and grab your sneakers and a camera. West Caicos is not for divers only. An eerily uninhabited island, beachcombers will revel in the white sand beaches that stretch endlessly along the eastern and northern shores. The tranquil solitude and quiet is unbroken except by the thunder of waves breaking on the shore or the shrill call of the island's avian residents. West Caicos also has its own unique history. Topped stone houses crowned by an osprey's nest, crumbling walls, a rusted railroad engine, and twisted tracks bear the last memories of a once bustling sisal and salt industry that operated on the island from 1890 to 1920. The stark, rugged cliffs on the western shore at one time provided protection for pirates and later for cruising U-boats. Today, wild flamingos, ospreys, and herons find a sanctuary at Lake Catherine, which dominates the center of West Caicos. The photo opportunities are abundant, so bring plenty of film.

The ruins of an old stone house now provide a perfect nesting place for one of West Caico's resident ospreys.

Typical Depth Range:	35 to 110 feet
Typical Current Conditions:	Slight to moderate tidal
Expertise Required:	Novice with instructor or divemaster
Access:	Boat

Sharks, grouper, black durgeons and wrasse make the Driveway their home. Beneath the mooring and the boat at 35 to 45 feet, a sandy area marked with scattered coral heads leads to a sand chute that slopes from 50 feet down through the reef, isolating a plateau that slopes from about 80 to 110 feet before a vertical wall plunges downward to the sea bottom. The plateau displays excellent and abundant examples of plate coral and mountainous star coral that create nooks and crannies in which lobster hide and an elusive orange ball anemone might conceal itself. All along the wall hang wire and black coral trees, while brown and purple tube sponges and brown antler sponges dot this vertical seascape with striking shapes.

The corals and sponges as well as the invertebrate life on the coral heads on the top reef make this a good site for night diving. Octopus and Caribbean spider crabs frequently make an exciting appearance after dark.

Purple and yellow sponges provide a brilliant accent of color on the wall at the Driveway.

Typical Depth Range:	50 to 130 feet
Typical Current Conditions:	Mild to moderate tidal flow
Expertise Required:	Novice top of wall; Novice with instructor or divemaster on the wall.
Access:	Boat

If you look toward the shore from the boat when you are moored at this site, you will immediately understand the origin of its name, White Face, because the shoreline is fringed by steep white cliffs that drop to the sea.

Descending from boat to the reef will reveal a white sandy bottom punctuated by a generous scattering of coral heads and a very lush top

Black coral trees grow quite large on the deeper sections of the walls in West Caicos.

reef that extends to the wall. There are several regal stands of pillar coral on the top reef, and not too far from the boat houses, there's a resident spotted drum. Schooling jacks patrol the area which is also frequented by barracuda, supermale parrot fish, a juvenile spotted drum, French angels, Nassau grouper, and a host of colorful tropical fish.

Just north of the mooring is a crack in the wall in which a large sponge-encrusted anchor is firmly embedded at 70 feet. Just behind the anchor is a swimthrough that is roomy enough for divers. But be careful not to stir up the silt on the bottom and on the coral under the arch. Other divers may want to enjoy this picturesque spot as well. The big purple rope sponge that dangles precariously at the edge of the crack makes a nice photo opportunity.

To locate the anchor, look for the buoy that marks the beginning of the crack. It is not too far from the mooring and you should get your bearings on the surface before you submerge. When the visibility is at its best, you can sometimes see the crack well before you approach. The fluke of the anchor has a purple tube sponge growing on it.

The wall is steeply vertical and undercut to about 100 feet when it begins to terrace more gradually as it descends to the depths. The top of the larger buttressing wall is covered with deep water gorgonians and small black coral trees, while large black coral trees identify the base of the mini-wall. Brown antler sponges, purple tube and rope sponges, and medium-sized barrel sponges can be found all over the face of the wall.

At White Face, schools of fairy basslets dart playfully among the coral heads.

Typical Depth Range:	45–65 feet
Typical Current Conditions:	Slight tidal current less than ½ knot
Expertise Required:	Novice with instructor or divemaster
Access:	Boat

Sunday Service is often visited for a warm-up dive and is excellent for novice divers. Unlike many of the dive sites in West Caicos, the wall begins around 65 feet and slopes gradually, and it can be enjoyed without descending too deeply.

Three sand chutes lead to the top of the wall where small coral heads shelter a wide variety of small creatures. Varied soft corals, yellow tube sponges, pillar coral, and star and brain coral create a textured carpet on the top reef while schools of goat fish, black durgeon, yellowtail jacks, schools of blue chromis, and barracuda cruise nearby. You are likely to see an occasional turtle in this area and, if you look closely at the sandy areas around the coral heads, you will be tantalized by the yellow-headed jaw fish that dart elusively in and out of their holes.

There is a good variety here for fish study. All the representatives from the Hamlet family including black, indigo, shy, and golden hamlets, white spotted filefish, black durgeons; the butterfly fish clan including spotfin, banded, and four-eye species; as well as fairy basslets congregate here. Because it is a fairly shallow depth for this area, divers will enjoy ample bottom time to familiarize themselves with this active marine community.

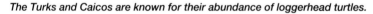

The Turks and Caicos are known for their abundance of loggerhead turtles.

Typical Depth Range:	42 to 115 feet
Typical Current Conditions:	Tidal up to 1 knot on occasion
Expertise Required:	Novice with instructor or divemaster
Access:	Boat

Isle's End lies at the south end of West Caicos where the tidal current tends to be a little stronger because it flows around the end of the island. Although at times it may be a slight inconvenience to divers, this current feeds the reef and that is why there are so many soft corals on the top plateau at this site.

Check with your divemaster as to the current conditions. They should not present a serious problem. Swim into the current when you begin your dive and with it on the way back when you are a little more tired and lower on air. If you have any concerns, there is plenty to explore right in the area below the boat and the mooring!

The dominant feature of the area below the boat is a large stand of pillar coral that sits in 42 feet of water. In general, the meadow-like terrain is rolling and meandering. A large plateau isolated by surrounding sand is an excellent place to see yellow tube sponges, sea plumes, rope sponges, and barrel sponges. Clouds of silversides move across the reef. There are coral overhangs along one of the sand chutes with huge snapper inside, large sea cucumbers crawling in the sand, and schools of goatfish grazing in the sandy areas as well. This is also a good spot to see loggerhead and hawksbill turtles and squid in the shallow area. Angelfish, trumpetfish, sand divers, and sand tilefish are also found at this site.

The sometimes strong tidal currents at Isle's End account for the lush and colorful marine growth that results from constant flow of nutrients.

5

Smart, Safe Diving

Preparation

Before you leave home, make sure all of your dive gear is in good working order and that all items that must be serviced yearly—especially regulators—have been. There is nothing as aggravating as getting on the boat, arriving on your first dive site, only to discover that your octopus is free-flowing. If you wear a mask with a prescription or have trouble finding a mask that fits you correctly, bring a backup mask. Masks have been known to arrive at a different destination than you, fall overboard, or break. You won't be comfortable with a borrowed mask if you can't see or if it keeps leaking. Finally, if you haven't been diving for six months or more, especially if you have logged fewer than 20 dives, it might be a good idea to take a practice or refresher dive either in a local pool at home or with an instructor at a dive store in the islands before you head for deep water.

A diver is careful to touch only dead coral to steady herself as she slowly approaches a resting loggerhead turtle.

Reef Etiquette and Bouyancy Control

While moorings may go a long way toward reducing anchor damage to our reefs, so far there is nothing to protect them from damage by divers—except divers. Dive sites tend to be located where the reefs and walls display the most beautiful corals and sponges. And it only takes a moment—an inadvertently placed hand or knee on the coral or an unaware brush or kick with a fin—to destroy this fragile living part of our delicate ecosystem. Only a moment can make a dive site a little less spectacular spot for other divers. Luckily, it only takes a little extra preparation and consideration to preserve it for generations of divers to come.

So if you're a new diver, a little rusty after a long hiatus on dry land, diving with new equipment, or if you just haven't paid much attention to your reef etiquette or bouyancy control in the past, here are a few helpful tips on how you can personally help preserve our underwater environment.

Weight Yourself Properly. Never dive with too much weight. (Northern divers—this means you! When you put on a lighter wetsuit or dive skin, shed some of those lead pounds, too!) Weight yourself so that you FLOAT AT EYE LEVEL on the surface with your lungs full of air and none in your BCD. Exhale fully and you should begin to sink. As your week of diving goes by and you relax underwater, drop some more weight. Ask your divemaster what kind of tank you're using. Tanks vary in their buoyancy when they are empty. You want to be able to hover comfortably at 15 feet to make your safety stop when your tank is low at the end of your dive.

Control Your Buoyancy with Your Breathing. If you are properly weighted and have successfully attained neutral buoyancy with your BCD at depth, you should be able to fine-tune your hovering capacity by inhaling and exhaling. Being able to rise and sink at will is the real trick to being able to hover, float, and glide over and around the reef formations with grace and skill.

Avoid Fin Damage to Coral. Never stand (or kneel) on the corals. If you're hovering above the reef, keep your fins up off the reef. If you're swimming, do so in a horizontal position looking down so you're not flutter-kicking the reef. When you're cruising through a narrow space such as a tunnel or gully between coral heads, keep an eye on where your feet are and, if necessary, make your kicks small and efficient to move you through the compact area. Reef etiquette also demands that, if your are swimming near a sandy bottom, stay several feet above the sand so you don't kick up any silt and ruin the dive for other divers.

Don't Touch the Reef. No matter how pretty and tactile the coral and sponges are, look but don't touch. And never, never grab onto the reef to steady yourself. If you need to stabilize yourself or keep from bumping into things or other divers, try using one or two fingers instead of your entire hand. And look for dead spots, areas between the corals or even the underside of a coral cranny where there is generally less growth.

Watch Where You Land. If you need to touch down or kneel on solid ground, look for a sandy area in between the coral heads. If you need to take a photo, float or glide over your subject or steady yourself with a finger, but keep the rest of your body away from the reef. If you can't get the picture or see your subject without lying on the coral, don't take the picture!

Don't Drag Loose Gauges or Octopus Across the Reef. Hanging consoles, goody bags, tools, and other unsecured equipment can do as much damage to the corals as your hands and feet. Keep your equipment close to your body by tucking them into your BCD pockets or using retainer clips.

Don't Grab the Marine Creatures. Don't ride the turtles, grab the lobsters, chase the stingrays, or harass the eels. They are curious by nature and will gradually move toward you if you leave them alone. If you grab them, they'll disappear faster than you can clear your mask— and no one else will have the chance to see them either.

Be considerate. Leave the reef in the same condition in which you found it. In this way, it will remain healthy and thriving for future divers to enjoy.

Hazardous Marine Life

Diving in the Turks and Caicos Islands isn't really hazardous. It's divers who are hazardous. When was the last time a stand of fire coral pursued a diver to sting him? Most stings, scrapes, and punctures are due to divers inadvertently bumping into coral or touching a creature that instinctively defends itself against its giant aggressor. Some injuries are harmless and merely uncomfortable. Others may require medical attention. Ideally, we shouldn't touch anything underwater, but it does happen and it does hurt!

Watch out for the following:

Fire Coral. Mustard brown in color, fire coral is most often found in shallower waters encrusting dead gorgonians or coral. Contact causes a burning sensation that lasts for several minutes and sometimes causes red welts on the skin. If you rub against fire coral, do not try to rub the affected area as you will spread the small stinging particles. Upon resurfacing, apply meat tenderizer to relieve the sting and then antibiotic cream. Cortisone cream can also reduce any inflammation.

Sponges. They may be beautiful but sponges can also pack a powerful punch with fine spicules that sting on contact. While bright reddish-brown ones are often the stinging kind, familiarly called dread red, they are not the only culprits. If you touch a stinging sponge, scrape the area with the edge of your dive knife. Home remedies include mild vinegar or ammonia solutions to ease the pain, but most of it will subside within a day. Again, cortisone cream might help.

Sea Urchins. The urchin's most dangerous weapon is its spines, which can penetrate neoprene wetsuits, booties, and gloves with ease. You'll know you've been jabbed from the instant pain. Urchins tend to be more common in shallow areas near shore and come out of their shelters under coral heads at night. If you are beach diving, beware of urchins that may be lying on the shallow reef you have to cross to reach deeper water. Don't move across it on your hands and knees and start swimming as soon as possible. Injuries should be attended to as soon as possible because infection can occur. Minor punctures require removal of the spine and treatment with an antibiotic cream. More serious ones should be looked at by a doctor.

Bristle Worms. Bristle worms make a great subject for macro photography, but don't touch them to move them to the perfect spot. Use a strobe arm or dive knife. Contact will result in tiny stinging bristles being embedded in the skin and resulting in a burning feeling or welt. You can try to scrape the bristles off with the edge of a dive knife. Otherwise, they will work themselves out within a few days. Again, cortisone cream can help minimize any inflammation.

Fire coral may look like dead coral, but it packs a sensational sting if touched.

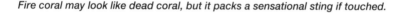

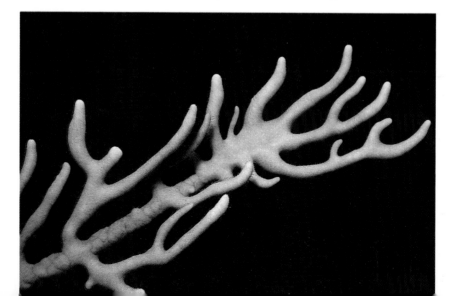

Sea Wasps. A potentially serious diving hazard, sea wasps are small, potent jellyfish with four stinging tentacles, and they generally swim within a few feet of the surface at night. If sea wasps have been spotted in the water where you are planning to do a night dive, take caution. Don't linger on the surface upon entry into the water. When you return, turn your dive light off as it attracts them and exit the water as quickly as possible. Their sting is very painful and leaves a red welt as a reminder. Do NOT try to push them away from your area of ascent by sending air bubbles to the surface from your regulator. The bubbles may break off their tentacles and you won't be able to see where the stinging tentacles are. If you are allergic to bee stings and sea wasps have been spotted at the dive site, consider foregoing the dive as you will most likely have the same reaction to a sea wasp sting.

Stonefish. They may be one of the sea's best camouflaged creatures, but if you receive a puncture by the poisonous spines that are hidden among its fins, you'll know you've found a stonefish. They tend to lie on the bottom or on coral, so, unless you are lying on the bottom or on the reef—which you shouldn't be (see "Reef Etiquette and Buoyancy Control")—they shouldn't present a problem. Should you get stung, go to a hospital or a doctor as soon as possible because the sting can result in severe allergic reactions, and pain and infection are almost guaranteed.

Stingrays. These creatures are harmless unless you sit or step on them. If you harass them, you may discover the long, barbed stinger located at the base of the tail which can cause a very painful wound that can be deep and become infected. If you suffer from a sting, go to a hospital or seek a doctor's care immediately. But the best policy is to leave them alone, and they'll leave you alone in return.

Eels. Similarly, eels won't bother you unless you bother them. It is best not to hand feed them, especially when you don't know if other eels or hazardous fish such as barracudas or sharks are in the area. And don't put your hand in a dark hole because it might just house an eel. Eels have extremely poor eyesight and cannot always distinguish between food and your hand. If you are bitten by an eel, don't try to pull your hand away—their teeth are extraordinary sharp. Let the eel release it and then surface (at the required slow rate of ascent), apply first aid, and then head for the nearest hospital.

Sharks. Although not an extremely common sight for divers, when sharks do appear, it is a cause for celebration and fascination. As a rule, most of the sharks you will encounter in the Turks and Caicos Islands are not aggressive and will not attack divers. However, it is wise not to feed them or harass them. If you are unlucky enough to be mistaken for a meal, the nearest hospital is the most logical next stop.

Barracuda. Barracudas have a miserable reputation. In fact, they are somewhat shy although unnervingly curious. They will hover near enough to divers to observe what they are so interested in, but just try to photograph them and they keep their distance. You'll see them on almost every dive. Don't bother them—and they won't bother you.

Diving Accidents

Diving is a safe sport and there are very few accidents compared to the number of divers and dives made each year. However, occasionally accidents do occur and emergency medical treatment should be sought immediately. If you are diving with a local dive operation in the Turks and Caicos Islands, they will be equipped to handle any situation expediently. If a diving injury or decompression sickness occurs when you are on your own, here are some important emergency numbers to contact:

Divers Alert Network (919) 684-8111
Emergency 62333
Hospital—Grand Turk 62040
Recompression Chamber—Provo 64242
Menzies Medical Center—Provo 64242
Marine Search and Rescue 64645
Police 64645

Bullsharks are generally harmless, but divers should exercise a healthy respect for these unpredictable creatures.

Divers Alert Network/DAN. The Divers Alert Network (DAN), a nonprofit membership association of individuals and organizations sharing a common interest in diving safety, assists in the treatment of underwater diving accidents by operating a 24-hour national telephone emergency hotline, (919) 684-8111 (collect calls are accepted), and to increase diver safety awareness through education.

DAN does not maintain any treatment facility nor does it directly provide any form of treatment, but it is a service that complements existing medical systems. DAN's most important function is facilitating the entry of the injured diver into the hyperbaric trauma care system by coordinating the efforts of everyone involved in the victim's care.

Calls for routine information that do not concern a suspected diving injury or emergency should be directed to the DAN information number (919) 684-2948 from 9 a.m. to 5 p.m. Monday–Friday eastern standard time. This number should not be called for general information of chamber locations. Chamber availability changes periodically making obsolete information dangerous at the time of an emergency. Instead, divers should contact DAN as soon as a diving emergency is suspected.

Hyperbaric treatment and air ambulance service can be costly. All divers who have comprehensive medical insurance should check to make sure that hyperbaric treatment and air ambulance services are adequately covered internationally. DAN membership includes insurance coverage specifically for dive injuries. Four different membership levels offering four different levels of coverage are available.

Membership ranges from $25 to $45 a year, which includes dive accident insurance; the DAN Underwater Diving Accident Manual, which summarizes each type of major diving injury and outlines procedures for initial management and care of the victim; a membership card listing diving-related symptoms and DAN's emergency and non-emergency phone numbers; decals with DAN's logo and emergency number; and *Alert Diver,* a newsletter that provides information on diving medicine and safety in layman's language. Special memberships for dive stores, dive clubs, and corporations are available. The DAN Manual as well as membership information and applications can be obtained from the Administrative Coordinator, National Diving Alert Network, Duke University Medical Center, Box 3823, Durham, NC 27710.

When the infrequent injury does occur, DAN is prepared to help. DAN support currently comes from diver membership and contributions from the diving industry. It is a legal nonprofit public service organization and all donations are tax deductible.

Appendix 1

Diving Operations

This list is included as a service to the reader. The publisher has made every effort to make this list accurate at the time the book was printed. This list does not constitute an endorsement of these operators and dive shops. If operators/owners wish to be included in future reprints/editions, please contact Pisces Books, P.O. Box 2608, Houston, Texas 77252-2608.

Grand Turk

Blue Water Divers
P.O. Box 124
Grand Turk
(800) 328-2288,
(809) 946-2432 (phone/fax)

International Diving and Watersports
Governors Beach
Grand Turk
(800) 866-DIVE,
(809) 946-2059 (phone/fax)

Off the Wall Divers
P.O. Box 177
Grand Turk
(809) 946-2159/2055,
(809) 946-2911 (fax)

Omega Diving International
67 Duke Street
Grand Turk
(800) 255-1966, (809) 946-2978, (305) 238-3039,
(809) 946-2877 (fax)

North Caicos

Dolphin Cay Divers
(809) 946-7119

Providenciales

Club Med Turkoise
c/o Club Med Sales, Inc.
40 West 57th St.
New York, N.Y. 10019
(800) CLUB-MED

Dive Provo
At Ramada Turquoise Reef Hotel
Providenciales
(800) 234-PROVO, (305) 359-2734

Provo Turtle Divers
Turtle Cove
Providenciales
(800) 328-5285, (809) 946-4232, (809) 941-5296 (fax)

Provo Undersea Adventures/Flamingo Divers
Turtle Cove Landing
Providenciales
(800) 327-8150, (305) 763-2188, (809) 946-4193 (Phone/fax)

Salt Cay

Porpoise Divers
Mt. Pleasant Guest House
Salt Cay
(800) 441-4419,
(809) 946-6927 (phone/fax)

Live-aboards

Aquanaut
Grand Turk
(800) DIV-XPRT, (809) 946-2541

Ocean Outback
Providenciales
(305) 923-DIVE, (809) 946-4393

Sea Dancer/Peter Hughes Diving
Providenciales
(800) 932-6237, (305) 669-9391,
(305) 669-9475 (fax)

Turks and Caicos
Aggressor/Aggressor Fleet
Providenciales
(800) 348-2628

Appendix 2

Further Reading

Barnes, Robert D., *Invertebrate Zoology,* Saunders College/Holt, Rinehart and Winston, Philadelphia, Pa., 1980.

Colin, P., *Caribbean Reef Invertebrates and Plants,* T.F.H. Publishing Co., Neptune City, N.J., 1987.

Gascoine, Bob, *Diving, Snorkeling, and Visitor's Guide to the Turks and Caicos Islands,* Graphic Reproductions, Miami, 1991.

Greenberg, I. and J., *Waterproof Guide to Corals and Fishes,* Seahawk Press, Miami, Fl., 1977.

Humann, Paul, *Reef Creature Identification,* New World Publications, Jacksonville, Fl. 1992.

Humann, Paul, *Reef Fish Identification,* New World Publications, Jacksonville, Fl. 1989.

Humfrey, Michael, *Sea Shells of the West Indies,* Collins, London, England, 1975.

Kaplan, Eugene H., *A Field Guide to Coral Reefs,* Houghton Mifflin Company, Boston, Ma. 1982.

Meinkoth, Norman A., *The Audubon Society Field Guide to North American Seashore Creatures,* Knopf, New York, N.Y., 1981.

Pisces Photo Pak of Caribbean Reef Fish, Pisces Books, Houston, Texas, 1990.

Rosenberg, Steve and John Ratterree, *Pisces Guide to Shooting Underwater Video,* Pisces Books, Houston, Texas, 1991.

Wilson R. and J., *Watching Fishes: A Guide to Coral Reef Fish Behavior,* Pisces Books, Houston, Texas 1985/1992.

Index